BY JAMES P. WARBURG

BOOKS

RECENT PAMPHLETS

WESTERN
INTRUDERS

JAMES P. WARBURG

WESTERN INTRUDERS

AMERICA'S ROLE IN
THE FAR EAST

ATHENEUM *NEW YORK*

1967

INTRODUCTION

BY EDWIN O. REISCHAUER

We Occidentals, ever since Marco Polo, have been discovering and rediscovering Asia. There is some doubt, though, as to who really has been "discovering" whom. The Asians, for at least the last two thousand years, have constituted the bulk of the human race and for most of that time have been more powerful and, in most measurable ways, more advanced than we. Even in the sixteenth century, it was we who were drawn to the great wealth of Asia, not they to our small and still not very productive corner of the world. Subsequently, a rapid upsurge of Western technology gave us at least a superficial domination over much of Asia.

Despite some centuries of trade, war, and colonial domination, however, Western knowledge of Asia has remained very thin. The real discovery of Asia is only beginning. It is coming dangerously late, because the rapid shrinking of the world makes it important that East and West know much more about each other than they have in the past. When they know more, they may be able to develop some of the real understanding on which peace and sincere cooperation depend.

James Warburg has brought his keen talents and broad background in business, writing, and government service to this task of discovery. In this charming book, in fact, he presents the voyages of discovery of Asia of three generations of Warburgs. Interspersed with a sweeping view of world history, the relations between East and West, and America's role in Asia, are presented extracts from his father Paul's diary of a trip in 1893 along the coast of Asia to Japan, his own account of a family trip to Japan and nearby areas in the summer of 1966, and his twelve-year-old son Philip's essay on "What I Got Out of Our Trip." This mélange of history, foreign policy, and personal observation makes lively reading and offers a helpful diversity of viewpoints in looking at this *terra incognita.*

Awakened only recently to his own "woeful ignorance of Asian history," James Warburg determined that his children would not "grow up in similar ignorance of three quarters of the human race." The result was the family trip and this book. The history is admittedly that of an amateur—but perhaps all the more understandable for that reason by other amateurs. The insights are those of a man of broad experience and keen perceptions. Many whose fathers did not leave diaries of Asian travels and who have not had the opportunity for their own family trips of discovering will wish to share vicariously in this three-generation experience of the Warburgs. Some who have already discovered Asia will profit from James Warburg's special perceptivity.

Edwin O. Reischauer

FOREWORD

When my father was twenty-four years old, he fell in love —not with my mother, whom he had not yet met, but with Japan. The affair began in 1892–1893, when my father and two friends set out from Hamburg, Germany, on a trip around the world. The three young globe-trotters went by rail to Genoa and thence by the *Hohenstaufen*, half steamer and half sailing vessel, to Port Said and Ismailia. From there, after exploring Egypt without much enthusiasm, they proceeded to India and Ceylon, gathering somewhat mixed impressions of Great Britain's Asian empire. A brief visit to French Indochina was followed by stops at Portuguese Macao, Hong Kong, Canton and Shanghai and then several weeks in Japan.

China, in the process of being carved up by the European powers, was written off by my father without much expression of sympathy for its plight; he referred to it as "the gloomy Middle Kingdom." Japan, however, filled him with delight from the moment when he stood at the bow of his ship as it entered the harbor of Nagasaki. . . .

As far back as I can remember, a set of samurai swords stood proudly on a carved teak chest in my father's study. No one was permitted to touch them, although one might carefully examine other treasured memorabilia of his visit to Japan. I recall one occasion on which my father drew the shorter of the two swords from its beautifully lacquered scabbard and explained to a guest how, in certain circumstances, a noble samurai would feel compelled to use this instrument to commit the unlovely act of hara-kiri.

Later in New York, when I was eight years old, my father instructed me as to the course of the Russo-Japanese War, which he followed with avid interest. Frequently, on Sundays, we played with tin soldiers on the nursery floor—a fascinating series of games in which I was usually allowed to maneuver General Nogi's or Marshal Oyama's blue-clad and always victorious Japanese troops against Stoessel's and Kuropatkin's brown-clad Russians, obligingly prepared for defeat by my father. Christmas in 1905 brought me a model of Admiral Togo's flagship, the *Mikasa*, which I proudly sailed in the bathtub.

(My father was anything but a militarist, as I was to learn later. At this time, however, he seemed to me as fascinated as I was with bringing about the annihilation of the Tsar's forces. I did not know then that M. M. Warburg & Co. in Hamburg and Kuhn, Loeb & Co. in New York—in both of which my father was a partner—had floated Japanese war loans, partly out of sympathy for Japan but perhaps even more because of antipathy toward Tsarist Russia and its anti-Jewish pogroms.)

To celebrate Japanese victory and the conclusion of the Peace of Portsmouth, largely engineered by President Theodore Roosevelt, my parents gave one of their rare parties. All the guests wore Japanese costumes; the entire house was decorated with cherry blossoms; and refreshments were served in a replica of a Japanese teahouse erected in the hall.

Shortly thereafter Jacob Schiff, my father's senior partner in New York, in whose honor the party had been given, went to Japan, where he was royally received and given a decoration by the emperor. As a token of friendship and respect, the

Schiffs brought home with them Wakiko Takahashi, the teen-age daughter of the Japanese Minister of Finance. The girl was accompanied by a Japanese trained nurse, Suo San, and remained with the Schiff family for several years. As I remember, neither of them spoke a word of English when they arrived. (In 1936 Wakiko's father, Baron Takahashi, was brutally murdered by a group of Japanese military extremists. By this time my good father was no longer living; he had died in January 1932 without realizing that, by its invasion of Manchuria a few months prior to his death, his beloved Japan had embarked upon a course of conquest that would lead it and much of the world to disaster.)

Regrettably, my early interest in Asia and particularly in Japan was soon submerged in a typical Europe-centered American education, followed by a career in international banking, concentrated chiefly within the Western world. During these years I had little contact with Asia. However, working for Franklin D. Roosevelt in helping to prepare for and eventually attending the World Economic Conference at London in 1933, I had some interesting dealings with Asian leaders, notably with the Japanese Foreign Minister, Viscount Ishii, and Mr. Eigo Fukai, governor of the Bank of Japan. Work on monetary and trade policies also brought me into contact with China's Foreign Minister, the lively Harvard-educated T. V. Soong, brother of the three famous Soong sisters— Mesdames Sun Yat-sen, H. H. Kung and Chiang Kai-shek.

Renewed government service in World War II in the field of psychological warfare, while concentrated upon the European theater, also brought me together with British and American colleagues concerned with similar operations against Japan. But it was not until 1947 that attendance at a Far East conference held at Stratford-on-Avon opened my eyes to the crucial importance of Western relations with the non-Western world, to the parochial ethnocentrism of Western society, and to my own woeful ignorance of Asian history. During the twenty years which have since elapsed, with the invaluable help of a number of good friends who are distinguished scholars, I have tried to fill in the gaps left in my one-sided education. More importantly, I became determined not to let my children grow up in similar ignorance concerning three quarters of the human race.

As a start in that direction, my family and I took a trip to the Orient in the summer of 1966. Outward bound, we crossed the Pacific by sea, partly because ocean travel will soon be a thing of the past, but even more because I wanted to use the leisurely days at sea to provide our four children with at least some background of non-Western history—enough to open their eyes to an unfamiliar world and, hopefully, to whet their appetites for further knowledge—at the very least, to make them aware that the world does not revolve around an Atlantic axis. Like most Western children, ours had learned, or were learning at school, little more than the history of the Judeo-Christian Caucasian civilization that spread from the Mediterranean Basin into Europe and eventually across the Atlantic. From their "social studies" they had learned a little about Egypt, and from the Bible they had become aware that another ancient civilization had flourished somewhere in the Near East. But they were wholly unaware that, centuries before the Golden Age of Greece, the rise of Rome and the beginnings of Christendom, highly developed and firmly established civilizations existed in India and China; and that, long before Columbus discovered America, not only had Japan and Korea likewise established distinctive civilizations in Asia, but also that, in America itself, civilization had existed for centuries among the Mayans in Central America and the Andean peoples of Peru.

Such a limited view of world history seemed to me of little use to a generation which, within its lifetime, would have to come to terms with a majority of the human race no longer willing to accept the supremacy of Western Man. Before taking up the main theme of this study—the confrontation of East and West—it therefore seemed desirable to summarize briefly in the first chapter the major developments in world history that preceded the first contacts between Europe and Asia.

To attempt such a summary obviously requires a degree of compression which does scant justice to the history of civilization. I have tried only to supply that minimum background of Asian history which should be but is not ordinarily provided by our elementary and secondary schools. (Although many of our colleges and universities now offer excellent courses on Asian history and Asian cultures, I question whether many of those who enter our institutions of higher learning without relevant preparation will be moved to embark upon a field of study in which their interest has not already been stimulated.)

The first chapter offers nothing more than an outline based upon the voluminous works of recognized authorities, some of which are listed as suggested reading. Since the presentation of such an outline of Asian history without its relation to Western history would be no better than the prevalent teaching of Western history without an Asian context, I have attempted to correlate the major landmarks of Eastern and Western history in such a way as to provide an overview of that part of the story of man which preceded the East-West confrontation. The same technique has been used throughout the subsequent, more detailed study of the centuries during which the West intruded upon the East; while emphasizing what happened in Asia, each chapter provides a brief outline of contemporary developments in the West.

Historians vary in their interpretation of the impact upon Asia of the Western intrusion, as well as in their condemnation or rationalization of colonial imperialism. My own view is that colonial imperialism was essentially predatory and based upon a wholly unwarranted assumption of the superiority of Western Man. I am not convinced that Asia benefited on balance from the Western intrusion, nor, for that matter, that the West benefited in the long run from seeking to dominate and, for a time, dominating the East. Be that as it may, history shows that, contrary to the belief widely held among Americans, the United States has not been innocent of the imperialism often attributed exclusively to the European powers. The fact is that, if mistakes were made and injustices committed in Asia by Western Man, we have shared in those mistakes and injustices, even though we were latecomers upon the Asian scene. As a nation, we have been and still are woefully ignorant concerning Asian history and Asian cultures. Along with most Europeans, we have lacked a decent respect for the peoples of Asia, considering them on the whole inferior to Western Man. In fact, Western Man has suffered from the same malady that caused the disintegration of the world's oldest continuous empire—the Empire of China. Like the Confucian Chinese, who considered their civilization superior to all others and their nation entitled to overlordship, we of the West have considered our civilization superior and our nations entitled to world dominance.

One by one, the nations of western Europe have now lost not their sense of superiority but their power to assert world dominance. The United States, on the other hand, has gained vastly in relative power and has acquired a sense of mission to preserve "law and order" in a world convulsed by ineluctable revolutionary change. There is danger in such an assumption of responsibility—danger to the United States and to all mankind.

This book has been written primarily for those young men and women of America who will soon have to deal with the problems left to them by ethnocentric forebears mistakenly convinced of Western Man's superiority and of America's mission, as the leader of the West, to police the world. It is they who will have to restore humility and a sense of proportion to the foreign policy of a well-meaning nation that has become somewhat dizzied by its sudden accession to apparently limitless but actually strictly limited power. Perhaps some of my unregenerate "Neo-Confucian" contemporaries may also find this study of our uninvited intrusion into the Far East of some interest.

As a Johnny-come-lately in the field of Asian studies, I cannot hope to do more than to serve up an appetizer. Perhaps the most important part of this book is the list of suggested reading.

The friends who awakened my belated interest in the Far East were: my wartime colleague Owen D. Lattimore; Wilma and John King Fairbank, whom I met at the Stratford conference in 1947; and Edgar Snow. Another good friend, O. Edmund Clubb, a former Foreign Service officer with vast experience in China, was good enough to give my manuscript a careful reading and to point out a number of errors and inaccuracies. Finally, I am most grateful to Edwin O. Reischauer, our former ambassador to Japan, for his charming and generous introduction; and to my publisher, Simon Michael Bessie, who had the happy idea of asking him to write it.

In drawing the maps contained in this book, I have relied upon a number of sources—chiefly upon those works which are listed as suggested reading, as well as upon the historical section of the *Rand McNally Cosmopolitan World Atlas*. If any of them are erroneous, the errors are mine.

My sister, Bettina Warburg, helped me in selecting the excerpts from our father's diary. My wife and our children contributed their impressions to the account of our own voyage of exploration. The manuscript was typed and retyped by Ruth van den Bogaert and Alice Madden.

J. P. W.

CONTENTS

MAPS

Designed by Ava Morgan

WESTERN
INTRUDERS

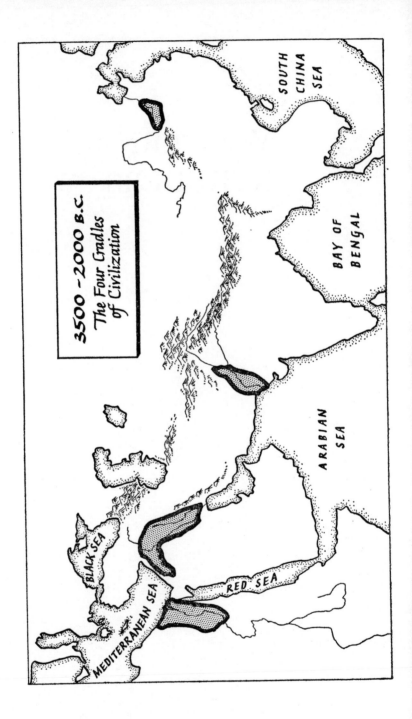

3500–2000 B.C.
The Four Cradles
of Civilization

SOUTH CHINA SEA

BAY OF BENGAL

ARABIAN SEA

RED SEA

BLACK SEA

MEDITERRANEAN SEA

1

East and West Prior to Their Confrontation

(To be skipped by those who know their world history)

I

THE EARLIEST CIVILIZATIONS

Human beings have probably inhabited parts of the earth for countless millennia, but civilization began only about 5,000 years ago when, in certain parts of the world, men who had been nomadic hunters settled down in small family or tribal communities to raise their food by cultivation of the land. So far as we know, this significant development occurred first in four widely separated great river valleys—the valleys of the Nile in Egypt, the Tigris–Euphrates in Mesopotamia, the Indus in western India and the Yellow River in north-central China.

The first civilized communities were small city-states which gradually acquired control of villages lying up or down stream, or outlying fertile areas inhabited by wandering tribes of huntsmen. Some of these city-states then expanded by gain-

3

ing control of adjacent similar communities until sizable kingdoms were formed. The earliest such kingdoms which grew into empires, probably about 3500 B.C., were Egypt and Sumeria.

Egypt

More than three thousand years before the Christian era, the cities and villages along the Upper and Lower Nile were united under the rule of the early pharaohs. These Egyptian rulers already commanded sufficient manpower and engineering skill to build the pyramids. The inscriptions, works of art, artifacts and records discovered in these gigantic tombs prove that a rich and well-ordered civilization existed at this time. Records were kept in hieroglyphics. Agriculture flourished. Weaving, pottery-making, wood and metal work had developed along with remarkable skills in mathematics, engineering and medicine.

In about 1800 B.C. Egypt was invaded and conquered by the Hyksos, a warlike tribe of Palestinians whose horse-drawn chariots overcame the pharaoh's foot soldiers. After about two centuries, the Hyksos were expelled, and, under a new line of pharaohs, the Egyptians conquered the whole eastern seaboard of the Mediterranean. This second flowering of Egyptian civilization lasted until 525 B.C., when Egypt was conquered by the Persians.

Mesopotamia

The Persians were the ultimate inheritors of a second, separate civilization which had arisen, also about 3500 B.C., in the

4

Tigris–Euphrates valley of Mesopotamia. So far as is known, this civilization was founded by a people known as Sumerians, who first settled in the Fertile Crescent, invented cuneiform writing, built great cities and constructed a remarkable system of irrigation. Whereas Egypt was vulnerable only from the north, the Sumerian civilization was surrounded by potential enemies who successively took over the area. Thus the Sumerians were overcome and succeeded by Akkadians under King Sargon and by other barbarian invaders who assimilated their advanced culture.

From 1600 to 1150 B.C. a Babylonian dynasty ruled Mesopotamia; then came the Kassites and, from 900 to 625 B.C., the fierce Assyrians from the north. Finally, a second Babylonian dynasty succeeded in establishing itself and ruled for about a century until Mesopotamia, like Egypt, fell under the relatively gentle rule of the conquering Persians.

India

At its height, the Persian Empire stretched from Egypt and the shores of the eastern Mediterranean to India, where a third great early civilization had developed in the Indus Valley. Its two major cities, Harappa and Mohenjo-Daro, may well have been as old and highly developed as Babylon or the Egyptian capitals of Memphis and Thebes, but this civilization left no written records.

China

The fourth of the great civilizations developed during the second millennium before the Christian era and had its origin

5

in the Yellow River Valley of China. While its earliest history is not reliable, it is fairly certain that pictographic script was invented before 2000 B.C., and there is archaeological evidence of considerable skill in the use of bronze and in silk culture during the Shang period, tentatively dated from 1766 to 1122 B.C.

During the succeeding Chou period (1122–225), Chinese civilization spread into the Yangtze Valley. The Chou kings ruled in the Wei Valley and gradually consolidated their control over a number of feudal states. By the third century B.C. there may have been some caravan routes into central Asia.

All four of these early civilizations developed as land empires in which the great majority of the population worked the land and performed other menial tasks under the direction of strongly centralized dictatorial governments that combined secular and religious authority. These land empires were essentially orthodox, status-oriented and resistant to social change. Their religions developed from polytheistic nature worship into various codes of ethics and various forms of ritual designed to reconcile men to the immutability of their fate and to acquiescence in higher authority.

Egypt was well protected by the desert which enclosed the fertile Nile Valley and, for this reason, preserved a greater continuity as an empire relatively free from invasion. The Mesopotamian, Indian and Chinese valley civilizations, on the other hand, were surrounded by militarized nomadic tribes and subject to frequent conquest or attempted invasion. The Chinese were particularly successful in defending themselves against barbarian neighbors and, in fact, often succeeded in assimilating them into their empire.

6

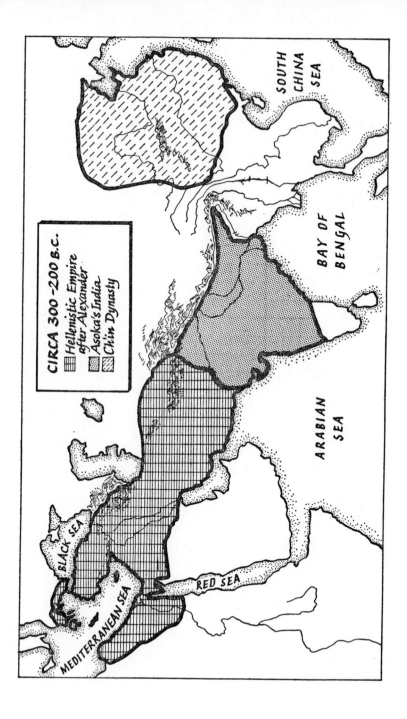

SOUTH CHINA SEA

BAY OF BENGAL

ARABIAN SEA

CIRCA 300-200 B.C.
Hellenistic Empire after Alexander
Asoka's India
Chin Dynasty

BLACK SEA

RED SEA

MEDITERRANEAN SEA

II

THE LAST 1,500 YEARS OF
THE PRE-CHRISTIAN ERA

During the last 1,500 years before the Christian era, two revolutionary developments took place in the Western world: (1) The Hebrew prophets, by proclaiming the existence of only one supreme God, opened the era of monotheistic religion—the era of Judaism, Christianity and Islam. (2) Travel by sea inaugurated the rise of maritime civilizations.

Greece

The earliest of these maritime civilizations originated in Crete and embraced the islands of the Aegean Sea. This well-developed civilization was, however, soon destroyed by Greek invaders from the north who absorbed much of the Minoan (Cretan) culture and founded the first lasting maritime empire. Moving out from their small mountainous homeland, the Greeks founded colonies along the northern shores of the Mediterranean as well as along the coasts of Asia Minor and North Africa. As a consequence of their overseas expansion, the seafaring Greeks became familiar with foreign languages, customs, products and techniques. This enriched their own civilization, widened their horizon and encouraged the spirit of inquiry, thus fostering the growth of individualism and a cultural flexibility sharply contrasting with the static orthodoxy and authoritarianism of the four great land empires.

Athens was the first city-state to encourage philosophical and scientific speculation, to recognize the value of an educated citizenry and to institute a democratic form of govern-

9

ment, even though Athenian citizenship was limited to a privileged class, with menial work being left to enslaved foreign captives. In the Golden Age of Pericles, there was a flowering of the arts and literature at Athens such as the world had not yet known, but this amazing cultural and domestic political efflorescence was not matched by sagacity in foreign policy. Athens wasted her wealth and energy in fruitless wars with neighboring city-states. Having twice defeated attempts by Persia to conquer Greece—at Marathon in 490 B.C., and ten years later at Salamis, the Athenians became military-minded and unwisely set about establishing their rule over Sparta, Thebes and other Greek cities which had been their allies. The resulting Peloponnesian Wars might well have brought about the end of Greek civilization, had not King Philip of Macedon come down from the north in 338 B.C., and forcibly united the warring Greek city-states.

King Philip's son, Alexander the Great, led the Greeks to an amazing conquest of the entire Persian Empire, from Egypt to India. Although, after his early death in 323 B.C., Alexander's generals carved up his conquests into several separate kingdoms, the third century before Christ became a century of Hellenistic civilization throughout the Mediterranean world and the Middle East.

Rome

Meanwhile, as Greek civilization spread eastward, a new power began to arise in the western Mediterranean. While Athens was in her glory, the Romans were quietly establishing control of the Italian peninsula. From there, like the Greeks, they set out to build a maritime empire. In this endeavor they were challenged by the Phoenicians who, coming by sea from Asia Minor, established Carthage in what is now Tunisia and, from there, threatened Roman control of the Mediterranean. In three costly Punic Wars (264–241, 218–201 and 149–146 B.C.) Rome finally disposed of the Phoenician challenge. During the same century, the Romans fought three successful wars against Greek Macedonia and five wars to conquer Greek-dominated Asia Minor. In 58–51, Julius Caesar crossed the Alps and conquered Gaul and Britain. By the time of his assassination in 44 B.C., Rome had become mistress of a Mediterranean Sea whose shores were ringed with Roman colonies and subordinate states or provinces. Rome had succeeded Greece as the center of the Western world.

This much of the history of Western Man in the last five centuries of the pre-Christian era is sketchily taught in most Western schools, although the emphasis is usually placed more upon military campaigns and conquests than upon the fantastic cultural development that took place in that era. The names of the Greek and Roman pagan gods are more familiar to most Western school children than the names of the great Greek and Roman sculptors, playwrights and poets, let alone the works of the great philosophers, astronomers and mathematicians. By the time Western children finish high school even this much of "ancient history" is usually forgotten, washed over by a flood of later material concerning their own particular nations.

As for Asia, most Westerners grow up with the notion that nothing much happened in that distant area until Western Man discovered and "opened up" the East. Yet the last millennium before the Christian Era was a time during which cultural developments were taking place in Asia which shaped

11

the nature of Indian and Chinese civilizations much as Mediterranean history shaped the ultimate nature of Western Man. (See map 3.)

Mauryan India

The information we have about India's early history is fragmentary. At about 2000 B.C., the early Indus Valley civilization appears to have been overrun by Aryan invaders from the North. (The name suggests a possible connection with the Iranians [Parthians] who invaded Persia.) Pushing the dark-skinned Dravidian natives southward, these Aryan invaders gradually extended their conquest across India as far as the valley of the Ganges. With them they brought their Brahman (later Hindu) religion, which, by about 500 B.C., crystallized into a rigid caste system. When Alexander the Great came upon the scene, a Nanda king ruled at Pataliputra (modern Patna) on the Ganges. A young relative of his, named Chandragupta Maurya, went to Taxila to study the means by which Alexander had been able to bring off his amazing conquests. Five years after Alexander's death, Chandragupta Maurya raised an army, drove off the garrison at Taxila left behind by Alexander and marched across India to overthrow the Nanda king at Pataliputra, thus establishing the Maurya dynasty. This was the first strong, well-organized government in Indian history.

During Chandragupta Maurya's reign, Seleucus, the general who had inherited Alexander's eastern empire, made an attempt to conquer India but was defeated by Chandragupta, who not only drove him back but captured most of Afghanistan, including Kabul and Herat. Chandragupta's grandson, Asoka the Great, further extended the realm by conquering the southeastern kingdom of Kalinga, thus bringing all of India except the southernmost tip of the subcontinent under his control. Unique among the historic conquerors, Asoka renounced war without subjugating the southern Dravidians. Instead, he became a Buddhist monk and made Buddhism the state religion, although he permitted proselyting only by peaceful persuasion. (Gautama Buddha had been born in India in 560 B.C.)

Most of what we know about Asoka's remarkable reign (264–228 B.C.) is derived from the chronicles of the Greek, Megasthenes, whom Seleucus sent as ambassador to Pataliputra. Many of Asoka's edicts have been preserved in stone and metal carvings. They preach against war and hold that the only true conquest is over men's hearts and minds.

About fifty years after Asoka's death, the Maurya dynasty collapsed and India was fragmented into warring states, a condition which continued during the years when Roman glory was at its height.

Confucian China Emerges

The sixth century B.C. was remarkable for its production of great thinkers, in Asia as well as in the Western world. Confucius and Lao-tse were contemporaries of Gautama Buddha. Their profoundly influential writings appeared in China during the long but uncertain hegemony of the Chou dynasty over something like one hundred warring feudal states.

Confucius endeavored to redefine and reform the feudal system, appealing for a restoration of China's legendary Golden Age, when wise kings were said to have established the rule of virtue and merit. Whether or not any such Golden Age had ever existed before 1122 B.C., when the Chou dy-

13

nasty was established, the fact is that, when Confucius wrote, the feudal system was dissolving into a period known as that of "the warring states." According to O. E. Clubb's apt description,* the distinguishing feature of the Chou era was the gulf existing between the feudal Hundred Clans and the "little folk," characterized by the saying: "Ritual does not extend down as far as the people, nor the penal code up as far as the nobility."

Confucius died in 479 B.C. The fratricidal conflict of the warring states lasted for 250 years before a centralized imperial government was established by Shih Huang Ti, the first Ch'in Emperor of China. (Hence the name China.) It was not Confucianism that brought about unification but the harsh logic of the legalist philosophers, under whose guidance the first emperor banned not only Confucianism but all other philosophical creeds, thus ending all free discussion.

Between 230 and 221 B.C., the Emperor Shih Huang Ti completed the Great Wall of China, built to check the "barbarian" invasions from the north. Even at this early date, the Chinese felt a strong sense of cultural superiority, looking down upon non-Chinese peoples as "barbarians" and expecting them to approach China as inferiors.

In 202 B.C. control of the empire passed into the hands of the first (Western) Han dynasty with its capital at Chang-an. Under the Han rulers, Confucianism was adopted and transformed to suit imperial rather than feudal purposes, and Chinese society and government first assumed their lasting form of organization.

This imperial Confucianism, designed primarily to fortify the centralized authority of the emperor, emphasized morality, respect for parental and ancestral authority, sane principles of

* *Twentieth-Century China* (Columbia Univ. Press, New York, 1963), p. 2.

statesmanship and, above all, intellectual attainment. It proclaimed the supreme authority of an emperor assumed to be both wise and good (although such was not always the case) and vested him with control over the moral behavior of society and defense of the realm as well as with authority over the crops, mines, currency and irrigation systems.

In foreign affairs, the Confucian concept of a universal empire sanctioned not only defense against barbarian invasion but the expansion of Chinese rule, either by conquest or by imposing a vassal status upon neighboring peoples. The subsequent history of China is one of expanding frontiers during periods of domestic peace, often followed by contraction during periods of domestic troubles.

Internally, the Confucian concept of government produced a theoretically benevolent despotism, with an administrative bureaucracy under the emperor composed of scholars and men of learning trained in government academies. In contrast to the Indian caste system, there was no hereditary elite, positions in the hierarchy being open to anyone capable of passing the scholarly examinations. Theoretically, a lowly peasant could enter the elite but only in the unlikely event that he could obtain an education and qualify by passing the examinations.

Agriculture was the primary economic activity and the chief source of imperial revenue. In theory, the Confucian system permitted a peasant to buy land from a landlord if he could accumulate enough money to do so. In practice, however, the peasant was at the mercy of the tax collector and the moneylender, so that the landlord was more likely to acquire ownership of the peasant's land than the peasant to increase his small holdings. This maladjustment in the tenure of land under the Confucian system tended to permit the concentration of land ownership in relatively few hands. Ultimately

15

the peasant's misery increased to the point at which he might be forced to sell his daughters. This led to recurring periods of banditry and peasant rebellion.

The other great weakness of the Confucian system, which was to show itself throughout most of Chinese history, was that it rested upon the assumed presence of morality and wisdom at the top of the pyramid of centralized authority. In practice, there was often incompetence, ignorance and corruption in the Imperial Palace, leading to internal rebellion, the overthrow of dynasties and periods of weakness and retreat in foreign affairs. Both the Han and, much later, the Ming dynasties were founded by leaders of peasant revolts.

In spite of these weaknesses of the imperial Confucian system, literature and the arts flourished under the first Han dynasty. Paintings of this period as well as exquisite, often humorous, sculptures have been found in tombs. The handicrafts produced fine lacquer work. Calligraphy on silk developed. Commerce expanded under the stimulus of government-maintained roads, canals and trade routes.

In the Year One of what we Westerners call the Christian Era, the people of the vast Chinese Empire were living under the most stable, skilled and sophisticated government the world had yet known. True, it was not a democratic government, but it was beginning to develop the world's first merit-based bureaucracy—the forerunner of the civil-service bureaucracies that were to develop in the West only a thousand years later.

Korea

The early history of Korea is largely legendary. A Tangun dynasty is said to have ruled from about 2200 B.C. until

1122, when the Chinese sage, Kija, is said to have founded the Kingdom of Chosen (Morning Calm) with its capital at Pyongyang and its realm extending from the Han River northward to the Yalu. Kija is said to have been followed by 42 kings in a dynasty which lasted until 193 B.C. In the south, two smaller kingdoms were founded at about this time —Silla, with its capital at Kyonju, and Pakche in the southwest.

CHRONOLOGY

I 3500 B.C. *to* 3000 B.C.

MEDITERRANEAN CIVILIZATIONS	EASTERN CIVILIZATIONS
First Egyptian dynasty in Nile Valley.	Neolithic Chinese civilization in Yellow River Valley.
Sumerian civilization in Mesopotamia.	First Indian civilization in Indus Valley.

II 3000 B.C. *to* 1600 B.C.

Egyptian kingdoms of Memphis and Thebes (2700–1800).	Legendary Hsia dynasty in China (*ca.* 2205–1766).
Sargon united Sumeria and Akkadia (2450–2270).	Aryans overran northern India, driving Dravidians southward (*ca.* 2000).
First Babylonian dynasty (1900–1600).	

17

III   1600 B.C. *to* 300 B.C.

Kingdom of the Egyptian Pharaohs. Invasion of Hyksos, followed by period of disorder. Jews enslaved in Egypt *ca.* 1300, led out by Moses *ca.* 1200 and settled in Canaan. Reigns of Saul, David and Solomon (1000–800).

Minoan culture in Crete (*ca.* 1800) destroyed by Greeks (*ca.* 1400). Formation of first Greek city-states (*ca.* 800–600).

Kassites conquered Babylon (1600–1150). Assyrians conquered Kassites (*ca.* 900) and Israel (*ca.* 800). Second Babylonian empire conquered Assyrians and Judah (600). Jerusalem destroyed in 500.

Rome founded in 753.

Persians conquered Babylon and Egypt, liberating Jews from captivity (525–500) but were defeated by Greeks at Marathon (490) and Salamis (480).

Golden Age of Athens ended with Peloponnesian Wars (431–404). Rise of Macedon (Philip unified Greece 338; Alexander the Great 336–323).

Shang dynasty ruled China *ca.* 1766–1122. Under Chou dynasty (1122–285) a feudal system developed. As the Chou dynasty weakened, China entered into the Period of the Warring States.

Northern India as far east as the Ganges was unified under the Maurya dynasty. Alexander reached Indus in 327. Asoka the Great halted further Greek invasion and extended his empire into Afghanistan and Baluchistan. Gautama Buddha born *ca.* 560; under Asoka, Buddhism became state religion, co-existing with Brahmanism. After Asoka's death in 228, the Maurya dynasty collapsed and India was torn by internal strife for five centuries.

Kingdoms of Chosen, Silla and Pakche were founded in Korea.

Note: During this period an advanced Mayan civilization developed in Yucatan and Guatemala. A little later (*ca.* 500) the Nasca and Chimu civilizations developed in Peru.

III

1 A.D. *to* 500 A.D.
India—the Gupta Period

After the breakup of the Maurya dynasty, the Indian subcontinent underwent five centuries of internal strife. There being no authentic records, the dates and areas from time to time

18

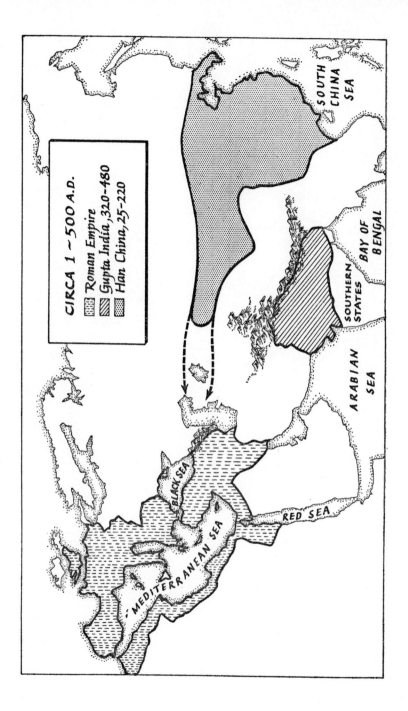

CIRCA 1 – 500 A.D.

Roman Empire
Gupta India, 320–480
Han China, 25–220

SOUTH CHINA SEA

BAY OF BENGAL

SOUTHERN STATES

ARABIAN SEA

BLACK SEA

RED SEA

MEDITERRANEAN SEA

controlled by the various competing states are in dispute. Early in the fourth century, however (about 320 A.D.), most of northern India was reunified by Chandragupta I (not to be confused with Chandragupta Maurya), who established his capital at Pataliputra, the administrative center of Asoka's earlier empire. Southern India did not become part of the Gupta empire. A Dravidian king, Pulakesin, established the southern Chalukyan empire, which is known to have exchanged ambassadors with the Sassanid rulers of Persia. Gupta rule in the north lasted for about two hundred years; Baladitya, the last Gupta king, died in 530 after his kingdom had been conquered by the Huns. The latter, under their savage leader, Mihiragula, remained in India for about fifty years.

The Gupta period corresponded in many ways to the earlier Golden Age of Greek civilization. Religious speculation, concepts of philosophy, ideas of law, mathematics, astronomy and medicine were vigorously pursued. Sanskrit literature flourished (the Panchatantra). Great universities were established at Benares, Taxila, Ajanta and Nalanda. A noted mathematician, Aryabhata, rivaled the Greek, Pythagoras. Charaka, a distinguished physician, recognized the existence of epidemics and described operations for hernia, cataract, Caesarean section, amputation and skin grafting. Rock sculpture represented both Buddhist and Brahman subjects. The mystical and negativistic implications of both Buddhist and Brahmanic thought gave Indian philosophy the unworldly and metaphysical intensity which has survived for centuries.

Han China

From 9 to 23 A.D. the rule of the Han dynasty was interrupted by the revolt of a powerful official, Wang Mang, whose socialistic reforms brought on a revolt and the restoration of the later (or eastern) Han dynasty. The eastern Han emperors ruled from 25 to 220 A.D. and greatly strengthened the centralized administration, shifting their capital from Chang-an to Loyang. Chinese influence was extended southward into Tonkin and Annam (now respectively parts of North and South Vietnam), and, under the Emperor Wu-ti (141–87), as far westward as the Caspian Sea, from where the Chinese silk caravans crossed the Parthian kingdom to reach the Roman Empire.

Buddhism obtained the sanction of the emperor and spread rapidly, rivaling the earlier Taoist and Confucian philosophies but not affecting the Confucian structure of government. Guilds of artisans that had formed in the cities of China began to fix prices and hours of work, and established quality controls. The guild, the family and the village council of elders governed locally. The artistocracy exploited the villagers under their control, and the vast peasant population lived by Confucian tradition, reluctantly paying taxes and showing but little concern with government.

Gradually the central Han government became unstable and from 221 to 265 China was split into the warring Wei, Wu and Shu kingdoms. The Wei (Chin) dynasty eventually triumphed and restored a loose union which did not, however, include the turbulent northern provinces or a number of minor dynasties struggling to establish their independence on the fringes of the Gobi Desert. This second, incomplete unification continued from 420 to 479 under the Liu-Sung dynasty.

During the first five hundred years of the Christian era, Chinese scholars visited Indian temples and monasteries, bringing back Buddhist texts. Some Taoist scholars ridiculed the formalism of Confucian society and adopted Buddhist ideas. Painting, however, continued in the Confucian tradition

22

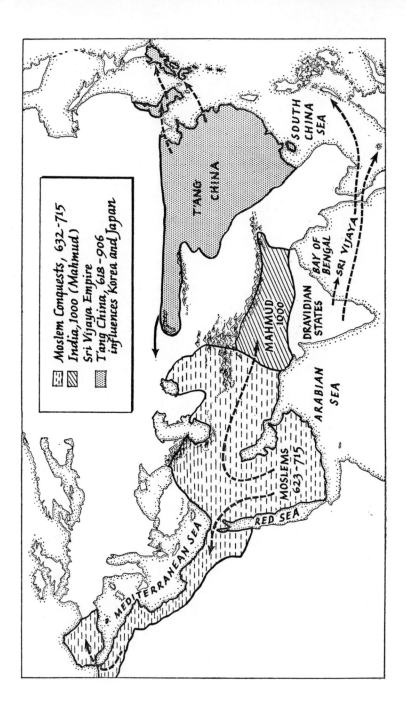

Moslem Conquests, 632-715
India, 1000 (Mahmud.)
Sri Vijaya Empire
T'ang China, 618-906
influences Korea and Japan

TANG
CHINA

SOUTH
CHINA
SEA

MAHMUD
1000

DRAVIDIAN
STATES

BAY OF
BENGAL

SRI VIJAYA

ARABIAN
SEA

MOSLEMS
623-715

RED SEA

MEDITERRANEAN SEA

and Wang Hsi-Chih, the greatest Chinese calligrapher, introduced the "one-brush" technique. Other artists transferred this technique to painting, using simple delicate lines and subtle shading. Music and poetry became closely linked. Shen Yueh, a poet, led in developing music as a separate art form and as a part of the dance program. Sculpture gained new impetus under Buddhist-Indian influence. Pagoda-building in honor of Buddha began.

Thus we can see that as Western Mediterranean-based civilization declined following upon the split of the Eastern Byzantine Empire from Rome in the fourth century and the subsequent Gothic invasions the Indochinese civilizations developed and expanded.

IV

500 to 1000 A.D.
Islam

The five centuries from 500 to 1000 A.D. were dominated in both Europe and Asia by the rise of Islam. Although, when he died in 632, Mohammed's influence was limited to the Arabian peninsula, his followers, fired with fanatic zeal, began a century of conquest that created a Moslem empire stretching from Spain to India. In incredibly swift succession the Moslems conquered Syria, Mesopotamia, Armenia and Persia; simultaneously they swept into Egypt and westward across North Africa, crossing the Straits of Gibraltar and occupying Spain. Here their advance was checked by Charles Martel at the battle of Tours, establishing the Pyrenees as the future boundary between Islam and Christian Europe.

In the Middle East, the Byzantine (Greek Orthodox) Christian Empire managed to survive but was narrowly confined in the Anatolian peninsula (modern Turkey), where it remained reasonably prosperous throughout most of the Middle Ages, while the isolated Christians of western Europe reverted to semibarbarism. Most of the former centers of Western civilization now lay within the Islamic domain. Even the Mayan cities in the as yet undiscovered Americas were more populous and prosperous at this dismal time than the shrunken and partly ruined towns of western Europe.

Ireland and Scotland had never been part of the Roman Empire. When the Roman legions were withdrawn from England, it fell prey to a series of Norse invasions. Angles, Saxons and Jutes destroyed the Roman cities and extinguished Christianity. By the year 600 the ruin of Rome's Britannia was complete. Celtic stock survived only in Wales and Cornwall. Augustine, sent by Pope Gregory I to win the Anglo-Saxons to Christianity, was partly successful but his work was destroyed by a new invasion of Danes, who were thrown out by King Alfred in 878 but returned in 991. In 1016 Canute, King of Norway and Denmark, made himself King of England. After his death in 1042, the English Kings were reestablished, only to succumb to Norman conquest in 1066.

On the Continent, the prosperity and progress achieved under Roman rule all but vanished. Roads fell into disrepair. Cities were abandoned and society disintegrated into isolated settlements. Only the priests and monks preserved Latin, the art of writing and the doctrines of Christianity. The growth of feudalism reflected the fragmentation of what had been an orderly empire, with only the Church of Rome preserving a semblance of unity. Charlemagne (768–814) attempted to unify western Europe and was crowned as Roman emperor by the Pope in 800, but his Frankish empire soon disintegrated; it had never reached much beyond the Rhine. Hemmed in by Moslem conquests, western Europe remained the prison of medieval Christianity until the twelfth century.

India Under Moslem Attack

In 740, north-central India had been substantially reunited by the Gurjara–Prathihara kings, who successfully turned back Moslem attempts at invasion. King Harsha, who died in 648, was the last of the great northern Buddhist rulers. During Harsha's reign, Arab Moslems penetrated into Sind and Baluchistan, but it was not until the year 1000 that northern India fell to Moslem conquest. In that year savage central Asian Moslems, led by Mahmud of Ghazni, invaded India and gradually extended their rule from the Indus to the Ganges. Southern India, however, remained free from Moslem conquest. Among a number of independent states, some Buddhist and some Hindu, Chola, with its capital at Badami, became the most important. Because southern India escaped Moslem destruction, many more examples of Indian architecture are found there than in the ravaged north.

Colonizers from the seafaring Dravidian states established Sri Vijaya—an extensive overseas empire that included Malaya, Ceylon, Sumatra, Borneo and the western half of Java. (Hindu East Java resisted Buddhist influence and eventually, in 1377, overthrew the Sri Vijaya empire, only to fall itself under Moslem influence.)

T'ang China

The Chinese Empire too had been plagued by discord and division for nearly four centuries after the fall of the Han dynasty in 220 A.D., until it was loosely reunited under the Sui and T'ang dynasties. But, unlike India, China escaped Moslem conquest. Under the T'ang emperors (618–906) a firmly centralized government maintained domestic order and resisted invasion; successful military expeditions, plus wise diplomacy, restored Chinese rule in central Asia and even brought Moslem Turkestan for a time under Chinese control. T'ang China's influence spread into Korea and Japan, with both Koreans and Japanese looking to and imitating Chinese culture. Tibet, lying between India and China, derived culture from both, accepted Buddhism and dominated a large central Asian area. Chinese influence spread into Tonkin, Annam and the independent Khmer kingdom of Cambodia, with its imposing new capital at Angkor.

During the T'ang period, Chang-an, now once more the capital of China, became a center of culture with a population estimated to have exceeded one million. Revenues were derived from the state-controlled salt and iron industries as well as from the taxation of peasants. The manufacture of porcelain, stimulated by the increasing use of tea, became a major industry. The silk industry prospered as more and more people wore silk garments. Paper money became a common medium of exchange. Half a dozen great Chinese poets wrote during the T'ang period, and at least twice as many notable painters produced landscapes, flower pieces and portraits. Block printing led to the production of the first books. Festival orchestras played over three hundred instruments. Popular music became an integral part of plays based for the most part upon historical stories and ancestor worship. Pre-Moslem Indian in-

28

fluence continued to find expression in the building of Buddhist stupas and pagodas. (See map 4.)

Korea

As China's influence spread into Korea, the Chinese helped the Kingdom of Silla to conquer the whole peninsula, overcoming the Kokuryo dynasty at Pyongyang and the southwestern Kingdom of Pakche. In 918, General Wanggum established the Koryu dynasty, which lasted until Korea was conquered by the Mongols in 1231. During the first five centuries A.D. Buddhism became the state religion in Korea and Chinese ideographs were adopted, although the Koreans used them to express a native phonetic language. Chinese at this time was the language of the scholars, fulfilling much the same function as that fulfilled by Latin in England at the time of Chaucer.

Japan Emerges

It was during the first five hundred years of the Christian era that Japan slowly emerged as a nation. Up to this time the four major islands (Kyushu, Honshu, Shikoku and Hokkaido) that were to compose modern Japan had been inhabited by the Ainus, a wild, hairy and savage prehistoric people said to have come from Siberia. Some of them survive to this day in the northernmost island of Hokkaido. At or about the beginning of the Christian era, a mixture of Korean, Chinese, Polynesian and possibly Indian people settled in the southernmost island of Kyushu and gradually conquered it up to the Inland Sea, moving from there to the southern part of the main island of

29

Honshu. (The smaller central island of Shikoku was apparently bypassed in this early migration.)

Legend has it that at about 200 A.D. the Japanese Empress Jingo conquered part of Korea.

Prince Shotoku, a Buddhist priest and regent for the later Empress Suiko (*circa* 600), played an important part in bringing Buddhism from Korea to Japan, as well as in adopting Chinese culture and an administrative system modeled upon that of China. (Shotoku's portrait is on the present-day ten-thousand-yen note.) At this time also, the Japanese adopted Chinese pictographic writing and, in 708, copper coins were introduced, probably from Korea.

In 710 the first imperial capital of Japan was built at Nara in the Yamato Plain. (Prior to that time each emperor had chosen his place of residence.) The Nara period (710–784) was noteworthy for the building of many temples, the emergence of official monasteries and the introduction of a code of law. Many of the beautiful Shinto and Buddhist shrines erected during this period remain to this day, some of them many times reconstructed.

In 794 the imperial capital was moved to Kyoto, marking the beginning of the Heian period. Kyoto was laid out in rectangles modeled upon the Chinese capital at Chang-an. The Heian shrine and many other temples in the beautiful city on the Kamo River show the strong impress of Chinese influence. Frequent embassies went from Kyoto to T'ang China during the Heian era.

Sung China

In 907 A.D., after almost three centuries of rule in China, the great T'ang dynasty collapsed, chiefly because of the devastating effects of a rebellion launched by the favorite of a dissolute imperial concubine. The collapse forced the withdrawal of the Chinese armies from central Asia and once more reduced the Chinese Empire to a shattered collection of warring states. The succeeding Sung dynasty never achieved a full restoration of the T'ang Empire, but under its somewhat loose rule Chinese culture was brought to its zenith, exerting its strongest influence upon the development of Japan.

Fujiwara Japan

From 866 to 1160 A.D., the actual rule of Japan was tacitly transferred from the imperial court to the powerful Fujiwara family, successive members of which acted as regents or prime ministers, often marrying their daughters into the imperial family and establishing something like a dynasty behind the nominal imperial rulers. Because the Fujiwara and other less powerful courtier families were permitted to acquire large tax-free tracts of land and, in turn, extended similar privileges to their followers, the Chinese concept of nationally owned land was never realized in Japan, and a feudal society developed that was quite different from the Confucian and highly centralized society in China. Instead of a governing elite of scholars there grew up in Japan an aristocracy of semi-independent feudal warrior-knights whose dominance was based upon shifting loyalties and military alliances.

While political authority was exercised by the Fujiwara during the Nara and Heian periods, a distinctive Japanese culture developed under the auspices of politically inactive although religiously venerated emperors. Poetry became an honored pastime at the Imperial Palace. The first Asian novel, *The Tale of the Genji*, was produced by Lady Murasaki Shi-

31

kibu—a romantic, delicately written tale of amorous adventure which emphasized both life's pleasures at the imperial court and the transitoriness of all human existence.

Thus, long before the western European nations existed as such, distinct national cultures had developed in India, China and Japan.

CHRONOLOGY

300 B.C. *to* 1000 A.D.

MEDITERRANEAN CIVILIZATIONS

Alexander's Empire broke up (300–200 B.C.) into Ptolemaic Kingdom of Egypt and Palestine, and Seleucid Kingdom of Asia Minor, with capital at Babylon.

Rome ruled Italy after 300 B.C., having conquered Samnites. Phoenicians challenged Rome and were defeated in the Punic Wars; Carthage destroyed in 146 B.C. Rome conquered Macedon, parts of North Africa, the Ptolemaic kingdom and that of the Seleucids. Caesar conquered Gaul and Britain. The empire reached its zenith under Hadrian (117–138 A.D.).

Rome declined. Constantine moved to Byzantium and adopted Christianity, making it a militant religion (308–337). Britain was evacuated 407. Western Roman Empire succumbed to barbarian invasions. Rome sacked 455. Byzantine Eastern Empire continued to flourish as western European civilization declined.

EASTERN CIVILIZATIONS

Shih Huang Ti became first Emperor of China in 221 B.C., ending Period of Warring States. The Great Wall was built. The eastern Han dynasty established in 202 B.C. Writings of Confucius (born *ca.* 560) were modified by the legalists and Confucian order of government and society developed. Empire was extended into Yangtze Valley. Expansion continued under western Han dynasty (25 A.D.–220 A.D.). Modified Buddhism sanctioned. From 221 to 265 China was split into Wei, Wu and Shu kingdoms, then Wei (Ch'in) dynasty established a loose union, lasting until 479. Sui (581–618) and T'ang (618–906) dynasties restored unity of empire. Chinese influence spread into central Asia, Korea and Japan.

Japanese civilization developed in first 500 years A.D. Buddhism was introduced from China *ca.* 600. Nara period 710–784. Heian period and Fujiwara dominance at Kyoto.

32

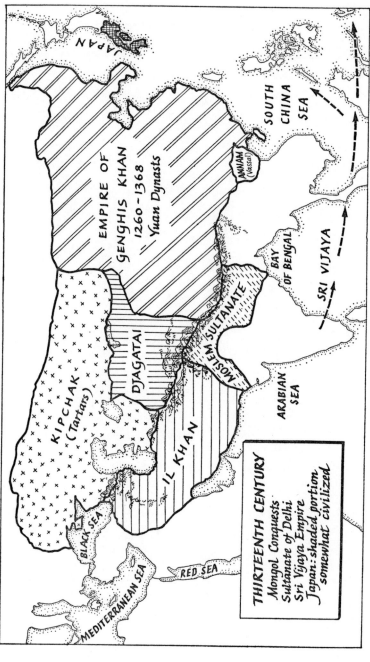

JAPAN

EMPIRE OF
GENGHIS KHAN
1260-1368
Yuan Dynasty

SOUTH
CHINA
SEA

AMNAM
(Vassal)

KIPCHAK
(Tartars)

DJAGATAI

BAY
OF BENGAL

MOSLEM SULTANATE

SRI VIJAYA

IL KHAN

ARABIAN
SEA

BLACK SEA

RED SEA

MEDITERRANEAN SEA

THIRTEENTH CENTURY
Mongol Conquests
Sultanate of Delhi
Sri Vijaya Empire
Japan: shaded portion
    somewhat civilized

MEDITERRANEAN CIVILIZATIONS	EASTERN CIVILIZATIONS
Rise of Islam began with Hegira 622. Moslems conquered Syria, Persia, Mesopotamia and Egypt in 632–642; besieged Constantinople in 678; conquered North Africa and Spain but were halted at Tours by Charles Martel in 732; penetrated central Asia and reached Indus in 715, but did not conquer India until 1000.	India, after five centuries of fragmentation, was reunified in 320 A.D. by Chandragupta I. Hinduism developed during the Gupta period, which lasted until 480, when India once more fell apart into warring states. In 740 the Gurjara–Prathihara dynasty once more united India and successfully resisted Moslem conquest until India was overrun by Mahmud in 1000.
Charlemagne expanded his Frankish kingdom into an empire and was crowned Holy Roman Emperor by Pope Leo III in 800.	

V

1000 A.D. to 1600

While western Europe stagnated in its narrow prison, Moslem culture flourished. During the eleventh century, Cordova, the western Moslem capital under the Omayyad dynasty, reached its peak as a center of culture and learning. A similar flowering of literature and science took place under the eastern Abassid dynasty at Baghdad. However, late in the eleventh century the power of Islam began to decline, especially in the East. The Seljuk Turks captured Baghdad and extended their conquests from Anatolia (modern Turkey) to the Caspian Sea, but Persia and India remained in Moslem control. The Byzantine Roman Empire resisted Turkish conquest and crusading knights from western Europe began their attempts to recapture the Holy Land.

Up to the year 1000, Christendom had included only the Latinized remnants of the Western Roman Empire, but now the pagan peoples of Scandinavia, Bohemia, Moravia, Poland

and Hungary were won to acceptance of Roman Catholicism. The Iberian peninsula was slowly recaptured from the Moors. The Russian Slavs organized the Kiev-Novgorod state and accepted the Greek Orthodox faith of Byzantium, now renamed Constantinople. Feudal warriors from western Europe launched the Crusades, and for a time regained possession of Jerusalem and the Holy Land. In the course of the Fourth Crusade, western Europeans, spurred on by the ambitions of the rising city-states of Genoa and Venice, established themselves at the Byzantine capital.

Within western Europe, centralized territorial states were gradually emerging. France, under the descendants of Hugh Capet (987–996) became a growing kingdom. England, conquered by the Normans in 1066, was slowly consolidated under the Plantagenet kings. As the Moors retreated from Spain, the kingdoms of Castile, Portugal, Catalonia and Aragon took shape. In the north, the German port-cities of Hamburg, Bremen, Luebeck, Stettin and Danzig formed the Hanseatic League. Trade throughout western Europe revived with the Crusades and the emergence of Venetian and Genoese sea power. Largely under the influence of the Church, western European culture began to blossom. Gothic cathedrals were built, such as Winchester, Chartres and Notre Dame. Scholasticism developed a system of logic and syllogistic argument. Moses Maimonides, the great Jewish philosopher, combined Jewish theology with an Aristotelian defense of scientific investigation, opposing the dogmatic fundamentalism of the Roman Church. The writings of Thomas Aquinas appeared.

Slowly, western Europe was catching up to Asia.

The Mongol Conquests

As western Christendom found new vitality and as Moslem power was slowly shrinking, a wholly new and powerful force arose in the Asian world of the thirteenth century. Moving out from their home in the steppes northwest of China, the Mongols, under their fabulous leader Genghis Khan, embarked upon a spectacular conquest which took them eventually from the Pacific to the Persian Gulf and from Korea to Hungary and Poland. These Mongol invaders were hardy mounted warriors, armed and trained from youth to hunt in great encircling movements and then to slaughter their surrounded quarry. In their extraordinary march of conquest, they applied the same tactics, sending out scouting parties to locate the opposing forces and then enveloping and destroying them.

Moving southeastward, they conquered the northern part of a divided China, then under Ch'in rule. At the same time, Genghis Khan's horsemen swept westward across central Asia to the Middle East, capturing Bokhara, Samarkand, Nishapur and Herat. Between 1237 and 1241 Genghis Khan's successor, Ogodei, penetrated into Hungary, Poland and the Balkans after overrunning southern Russia. In 1258 Baghdad fell to the invaders. A few years later Genghis Khan's grandson, Kublai Khan, conquered the southern Sung empire and united all of China and Korea under the Mongol Yuan dynasty.

The whole Islamic world was thrown into confusion. Mongol raiding parties were sent into northern India and even into the Indonesian islands. Although the destruction wrought by the Mongols blighted Asian civilization for a time, their conquests had curiously few permanent results. China remained under a Mongol dynasty for almost a century but the Chinese assimilated their conquerors and maintained their own culture and institutions. Most of northern India fell under Mongol rule, but here, as in China, the invaders imposed no religion or culture of their own, leaving—apart from physical destruction—little permanent impact.

The sudden, swift creation of the greatest empire the world had yet known was like a tidal wave that left temporary havoc but little other change in its wake. The wave broke wherever it encountered dense forests in which the Mongol horsemen were unable to maneuver, or wherever their advance reached the sea. The greatest lasting impact was upon Russia, where Mongol (Tartar) influence left a permanent imprint upon the nascent Slavic civilization.

Japan Escapes Mongol Conquest

Toward the end of the twelfth century, the power of the Fujiwara declined as two other great clans competed for supremacy. The Taira (Heike) clan held power for a short period but were then defeated by their Minamoto (Genji) rivals. Minamoto Yoritomo, Japan's first great strategist, rose to power after his brother, Yoshitsune, destroyed the Taira forces in 1185 at the battle of Yashima Hill near Takamatsu on the island of Shikoku.

(According to accepted history, Yoshitsune was killed in battle, but an interesting and widely believed legend has it that he escaped from his jealous older brother's pursuit and fled to Siberia, thence to Mongolia, where he is said to have become the great Mongol leader, Genghis Khan. The legend is fortified by the fact that Yoshitsune's name in Chinese was actually Gengi Kei.)

Legend aside, it is a fact that Yoshitsune's brother, Yoritomo, set up a military government at Kamakura and was the first to assume the title of shogun (generalissimo). This *ba-*

kufu (camp government) at Kamakura had no legal authority whatever but was destined to rule Japan for the next 150 years. From 1189 to 1333 Japanese emperors maintained nominal rule at Kyoto via regents or prime ministers who lacked the resources to assert any real authority, while the actual power resided in the shoguns at Kamakura. The succession of shoguns who followed Yoritomo relied upon a loose association of feudal knights bound to Kamakura by personal loyalty based upon the allotment of widely scattered estates.

While this peculiar development was taking place in Japan, Genghis Khan's grandson, Kublai Khan, was consolidating his control of China. He built a new capital at T'aitu, and, having solidified his rule on the mainland, sent emissaries to Japan demanding its acceptance of Mongol domination. The weak imperial government at Kyoto was terrified and inclined to submit, but when Kublai's emissaries came to Kamakura, they were beheaded on the Enoshima beach where they had stepped ashore. Inevitably, this act of defiance produced a strong reaction.

In 1274 a Mongol force landed in northern Kyushu but withdrew when its Chinese-Korean fleet was scattered by a storm. To guard against a second invasion attempt, the Kamakura knights built a wall guarding the same landing beach, assuming, correctly as it turned out, that the thrust would again be made there. The wall, defended by the samurai, would not, however, have been sufficient to halt the second invasion, undertaken in 1281 with 150,000 men, had it not been for a second great storm (the *kamikaze*, or divine wind) which again scattered and destroyed the invading fleet. Victory over the dreaded Mongols stirred Japanese pride, but the long and costly effort drained the strength of the Kamakura nobles. Gradually their power waned.

In 1331, the Emperor Go-Daigo II made an abortive attempt to assert the long-dormant imperial authority, aided at first by a defecting Kamakura general, Takauji Ashikaga. At the last moment, however, Takauji switched sides, deserted both Kamakura and Go-Daigo, and enthroned a rival emperor at Kyoto under whom he assumed for himself the title of Shogun. The dethroned emperor fled to the south and for the next sixty years Japan had two rival emperors, while actual power resided in the Ashikaga Shogun at Kyoto. The Ashikaga or Muromachi period lasted from 1338 until 1573.

China Under Mongol Rule

China, meanwhile, prospered under the Mongol Yuan regime. Kublai Khan assimilated Chinese customs and culture and encouraged Confucian scholarship. His reign was noteworthy for improvements in communications and commerce and the expansion of the empire. Moslems, Buddhists, Christians and Jews were treated with equal tolerance. Trade between China and the West increased both by well-maintained overland routes and by sea. This intercourse brought to Western attention a number of Chinese inventions, such as paper, gunpowder and the mariner's compass. Marco Polo, who served Kublai Khan from 1275 to 1292, brought back to Europe many of these innovations, including the use of coal for fuel in place of wood. Silks and porcelains were shipped from Chinese ports to Java, Malaya, Ceylon, India and Persia in exchange for spices, gems and pearls.

An empire-wide system of schools was established. A large hospital was built in 1271 and welfare relief was extended to orphans, the aged and those in ill health. However, the Mongols had never been more than a small minority in China. In 1368 they were expelled from the magnificent capital they had built on the approximate site of the later Peking, by Chu Yuan-Chang, the first Ming Emperor of China.

Tamerlane Invades India

Although they had lost China and failed to take Japan, the Mongols were not quite finished. In 1398 Timur (Tamerlane) invaded India, sacked Delhi, murdered the Moslem ruler and then retreated to Samarkand, whence he had come.

Japan Under the Ashikaga

With the ousting of the Mongol dynasty from China and the advent of the Ming dynasty, Chinese influence again gained in Japan. Zen Buddhist monks began to establish an educational system and to assert political power under the weak Ashikaga shogunate. Under Chinese influence the arts once more flourished. The Noh drama was born under Zen tutelage, its purpose being to teach the concepts of Buddhism. Deriving from early religious dances, the Noh drama combined symbolic choreography with poetic recitations chanted by actors and a chorus. Many of the texts of these religious plays became a part of Japanese literature and have been kept alive by devotees throughout subsequent Japanese history. A typically Japanese art of landscape gardening developed and the stately tea ceremony was introduced. Japan began to develop a distinctly individual culture of its own.*

However, the Ashikaga period was one of almost constant internal conflict. The estates of the samurai warriors were

---

* At approximately this time Dante, Petrarch and Boccaccio were writing in Italy, while Chaucer's and Wyclif's work appeared in England.

41

gradually consolidated into a number of large domains ruled over by feudal lords, known as daimio. Because of the continual strife between these provincial rulers and the weakness of the shogunate, the later Ashikaga period is sometimes referred to as Japan's "Dark Age." Actually, in spite of political instability, the period was one of great economic as well as cultural progress. Foreign trade flourished as enterprising Japanese warrior-traders—some of them pirates—gradually gained control of the China Sea and even roamed as far as the East Indies and Southeast Asia. Osaka became a thriving commercial city dominated by the great Shin Buddhist monastery, which itself engaged in foreign commerce, chiefly with China. As more and more manufactured goods were imported into Japan, its townspeople learned the arts of manufacture and were soon exporting finished goods as well as raw materials. Because of their military prowess, Japanese were welcomed as mercenaries by the early Portuguese and Spanish traders. A sizable number of Japanese settled in Manila, and even in Siam. In the middle of the sixteenth century, Jesuit and Franciscan Catholic missionaries tried to bring Christianity to the island empire, vying with each other in making converts. For a time they were quite successful, especially in Kyushu.

All in all, Japan emerged from its so-called Dark Age as an economically advanced though politically backward country, quite ready to compete with China and the forward-thrusting Europeans. All it lacked to become a great nation was a strong unifying central government. As the Ashikaga period drew to a close, no one could foresee that Japanese unification would be achieved at the cost of two and a half centuries of self-imposed isolation.

The West (Fifteenth Century)

In science and technology the Europe of the fifteenth century was learning and still had much to learn from the older Asian civilizations; its industry and trade lagged behind those of the Middle East and China. Most of the goods Europe produced were not suitable for export or else could not compete in quality with Eastern products. As a consequence, western Europe as a whole suffered, as had the Roman Empire, from a chronically unfavorable trade balance which drained away its small stocks of gold.

Nevertheless, the fifteenth century was one of marked European progress, especially in the literary and artistic revival which began with the Italian Renaissance. Politically, too, western Europe was developing, with monarchical power gradually triumphing over feudalism. As the townspeople supplied more and more of the funds with which the kings overcame the disruptive power of the feudal barons, the alliance between monarchs and burghers led to the beginnings of representative government.

The revitalization and modernization of western Europe was, however, hampered by continued Moslem threats from the East. Constantinople had fallen to the Turks in 1453. The end of the Byzantine Empire opened all of southeastern Europe to Moslem conquest; the Black Sea became a Turkish lake and the lower Danube Valley up to and including Budapest, fell under Moslem control. Farther east, Persia, which had been ruled by the Mongol Tamerlane and his successors, was likewise conquered by the Turks in 1469.

Trade between Europe and Asia remained in Moslem control. As yet there was nothing to indicate that Europe was about to liberate itself from Moslem encirclement. Toward the end of the fifteenth century there was scarcely a sign of the huge outflanking movement that was about to begin by sea.

So much for the background of history leading up to the confrontation of East and West.

2

The Sixteenth-Century Advent of European Sea Power

Three Chinese inventions—the sternpost rudder, the compass and the rigging of sails which enabled vessels to tack against the wind—enabled the Portuguese, Spaniards and, later, the British and Dutch to build ships capable of making long ocean voyages. A fourth Chinese invention, gunpowder, made it possible to arm ships with cannons with which to sink hostile vessels and to bombard land fortifications. By adopting these Chinese improvements and combining them, the Europeans were able to conquer the oceans and to bring about one of the most dramatic reversals in the tide of human history.

The European Explorers

Between 1492 and 1552 Columbus discovered America, Da Gama sailed around Africa to India and Magellan's fleet circumnavigated the globe. These three voyages and others which followed marked the beginning of a new age. By establishing a cheaper and safer method of communication in place of the long and dangerous overland routes between East and West, the early navigators freed Europe from Moslem interference with East–West trade and, even more important, became the masters of the oceans which covered seven-tenths of the earth's surface. This enabled Europe to obtain from Africa and America the gold which it had lacked and, with the gold, to purchase the silks, spices, tea and porcelain of the East. Almost overnight, two of the weakest European states, Portugal and Spain, became centers of wealth and empire.

After the first voyage of Columbus, Spain appealed to Pope Alexander VI to delimit its own and Portugal's spheres of exploration and conquest. The Pope granted Spain exclusive rights to all non-Christian lands west of a line running north and south one hundred leagues west of the Azores. The Portuguese persuaded the Spaniards to move this line 270 leagues further westward (roughly to the forty-sixth degree west longitude by later Greenwhich reckoning). The Pope granted Portugal exclusive rights to discoveries east of this line, which gave it not only Africa, India, China and western Japan but also a claim to South America as far west as the mouth of the Amazon. Although the Philippines lay within the Portuguese sphere, they were claimed for Philip of Spain by Magellan and later colonized. Apart from this Spanish settlement in the Far East and the Portuguese settlement of Brazil, the two Iberian powers stayed for the most part in their two widely separated areas—Spain in the Americas and Portugal in Africa and Asia.

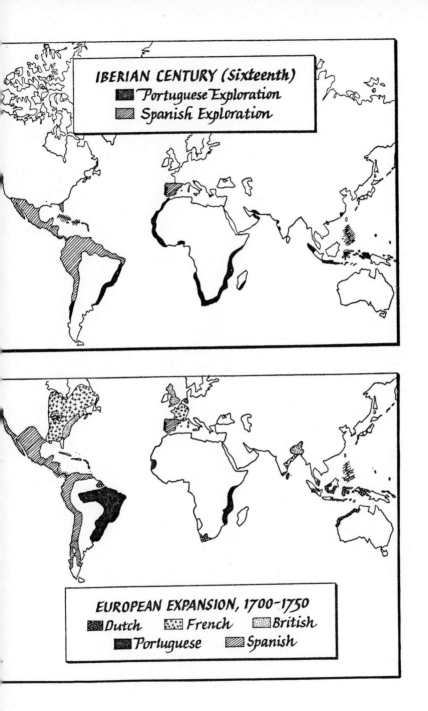

IBERIAN CENTURY (Sixteenth)
Portuguese Exploration
Spanish Exploration

EUROPEAN EXPANSION, 1700–1750
Dutch   French   British
Portuguese   Spanish

Portugal Invades Asia

In 1500 the commerce of the Middle East was still controlled by the Moslem Arab traders who sold the spices of the East to the Turks, who in turn sold them to the Venetian and Genoese merchants. However, when Da Gama returned from India with a cargo worth sixty times the cost of his voyage, the Portuguese set out to control the Arabian Sea, the Persian Gulf, the Indian Ocean and the Straits of Malacca. Within twenty years they were bringing the products of the East to Europe by sea. This eliminated both Moslem and Italian profits as middlemen in East–West trade and brought about the end of Venetian and Genoese days of glory.

Having established themselves at Ormuz at the mouth of the Persian Gulf, at Goa on the west coast of India and at Malacca in the East Indies, the Portuguese pushed on early in the century to seek trading posts on the coasts of China and Japan. Portuguese merchants and missionaries were admitted to Kyushu in Japan in 1549 and to Macao on the southern China coast in 1557. In India the Portuguese secured and fortified Diu (near Bombay) in addition to Goa and succeeded in warding off attempts to expel them. During this period Baber, a Moslem descendant of Tamerlane, conquered Delhi and established a Mogul dynasty in northern India.

The Iberian Era

Meanwhile, during the first half of the sixteenth century, the Spaniards conquered Mexico and Peru, bringing the two most cultured, rich and populous regions in the Western Hemisphere under their control. Aztec and Inca gold flowed to Spain from Mexico and Peru, while the Portuguese obtained a source of the yellow metal in Mozambique and inaugurated a highly profitable trade in African slaves.

The sixteenth century was the Golden Age of Spain. Charles V inherited from his maternal grandparents, Ferdinand and Isabella, the throne of Spain as well as Sardinia, Sicily and Naples and the newly discovered lands in America. From his father, King Philip, he inherited Burgundy, Luxembourg and the Netherlands; and from his paternal grandfather, Maximilian of Hapsburg, the Hapsburg territories in Austria and the Germanies. In 1519 he was elected Holy Roman Emperor. As such, he rallied the Germans to resist the Turkish advance in southeastern Europe and fought off French attempts to encroach upon his domain. However, the Holy Roman Empire was greatly weakened during the first half of the century by the Protestant revolt against the papacy, sparked by Martin Luther in 1517, which split the northern half of Europe away from the Roman Catholic faith. There was more than a religious aspect to the Protestant Reformation; the rulers of the northern states wanted greater power and more revenue, which they obtained by closing the monasteries and seizing Church lands.

Charles V abdicated in 1556. His son, Philip II, inherited the western parts of his vast realm, while a younger son, Ferdinand, received the Hapsburg dominions and was elected Holy Roman Emperor. Philip led the Catholic counterreformation, in which the newly founded Society of Jesus (Jesuits) became the spearhead. In Spain itself Philip caused the Inquisition to repress all non-Catholics, especially the Jews and the Moriscos (converted Moslems). When Catholic Mary Queen of Scots was executed by order of the Protestant Elizabeth, Queen of England, Philip launched his "Invincible Armada" against the island kingdom. Its defeat by the English and Dutch fleets marked the beginning of the end of Span-

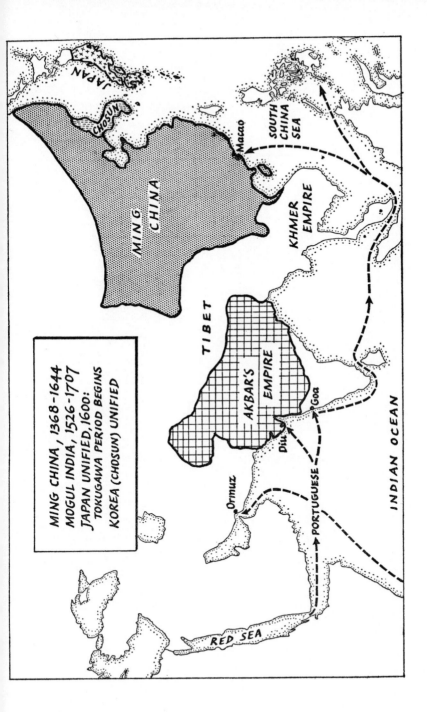

MING CHINA, 1368-1644
MOGUL INDIA, 1526-1707
JAPAN UNIFIED, 1600:
TOKUGAWA PERIOD BEGINS
KOREA (CHOSUN) UNIFIED

JAPAN

CHOSUN

MING CHINA

Macao

SOUTH CHINA SEA

KHMER EMPIRE

TIBET

AKBAR'S EMPIRE

Goa

Diu

PORTUGUESE

Ormuz

INDIAN OCEAN

RED SEA

ish supremacy, although the Dutch and Belgian Netherlands had already revolted against Spanish rule. From here on, English, Dutch and French sea raiders challenged the Spanish and Portuguese overseas empires, frequently intercepting shipments of gold from America and from Africa.

Korea

After the Mongol tide receded, Korea went through a period of disorganization until, in 1392, a strong government was once more established by Yi Taicho, who banned Buddhism, blaming the priesthood for the weakness of the Korean state. At about this time the Koreans developed their own twenty-six-letter alphabet by means of which their phonetic language could be printed. Fifty years before Gutenberg introduced the use of metal type in Germany, Koreans were using metal type instead of wooden blocks. An extensive Korean literature of this period included poetry as well as historical works. Under the Ming emperors of China, the status of Korea was that of a semi-independent tributary state.

Ming China (1368–1644)

The reign of the Ming emperors was marked by high scholarship and artistic accomplishment. During the sixteenth century the central government at Peking was less concerned with the appearance of Europeans in Asia than with intra-Asian affairs, such as Mongol and Manchu pressure from the north and west and Japanese attacks upon Korea. Christian missionaries were tolerated but made few converts; their arrogant assertion of religious dogma tended to alienate the Chinese.

During the reign of Emperor Shen Tsung (1573–1620), the dynasty began to show signs of weakening.

The Unification of Japan (1573–1600)

The long period of internal conflict under the Ashikaga shoguns came to an end with the appearance of three of the most interesting figures in Japanese history—Oda Nobunaga, Hashiba Hideyoshi and Tokugawa Ieyasu. These three men brought about the unification of Japan.

Nobunaga, a wily and ambitious daimio, who ruled the Nagoya (Kansai) region of western Honshu, deliberately set out to subdue the warring factions and to bring all of the daimio under his domination. More through guile and diplomatic skill than by the application of superior force, he gained control of Kyoto and, after a ten-year siege, succeeded in obtaining the surrender of Osaka Castle, the stronghold of the powerful Shin Buddhist sect. Two years later, before he could complete his conquest of Japan, Nobunaga was assassinated.

The completion of Nobunaga's work of unification was undertaken by Hideyoshi (later known as Hideyoshi Toyotomi), a common farmer's son whose devotion, skill as a spy and, later, as a field commander had earned Nobunaga's admiration and trust. A superb general, Hideyoshi proceeded to subdue the great Satsuma clan on Kyushu and then to defeat and destroy the Hojo clan that had briefly succeeded in displacing the Ashikaga shoguns. Next Hideyoshi conquered the northern "outer daimio." In the last battle of his campaign, he employed a characteristic stratagem to capture Odawara Castle, the seat of another and unrelated Hojo family. Having failed to reduce Odawara by siege and assault, Hideyoshi ordered the overnight construction of a sham castle, made of wood and paper, on a hill across the valley. The incredible feat of apparently constructing a fortress overnight so frightened and impressed the defenders of Odawara that they surrendered.

Not content with his domestic triumphs, Hideyoshi now dreamed of employing his powerful armies to subjugate the haughty Empire of China. In embarking upon this ambitious adventure, he made the fatal mistake of undertaking an overseas operation without a navy sufficiently strong to guard his line of supply.* The Japanese troops quickly overran Korea but, when they ran out of supplies and reinforcements, suffered defeat by the Chinese at the Yalu River. (For a time Hideyoshi held on, but after his death the troops were withdrawn by his successor, Tokugawa Ieyasu.)

Always conscious of his lowly birth, Hideyoshi endeavored to demonstrate that he was not only a great military leader but also a man of culture. In this he had some success. He encouraged the arts and fostered the promotion of the tea ceremony (which some say his chamberlain invented). For the emperor at Kyoto he built the charmingly tasteful Detached Katsura Palace, while at Osaka he erected the great moated fortress known as the Castle.

Familiarly called "the Monkey," partly because of his looks and partly because of his sense of humor, Hideyoshi left a rich heritage of true history and fanciful legend that formed the basis of much of later Japanese literature, painting and Kabuki drama.

* On land the Japanese had the advantage of possessing matchlock muskets as well as superiority in numbers. At sea, however, they were no match for the Koreans, who surprised them by opposing the Japanese vessels with ironclad vessels propelled by oarsmen. An early print shows that these forerunners of the armored warship looked like giant turtles, with eight long oars protruding like legs from each side.

Tokugawa Ieyasu was in many ways the most competent of the three unifiers of Japan. Coldly calculating and realistically ambitious, he defeated the last of the rebellious lords in 1600 at the battle of Segikahara. Then, determined to establish the lasting rule of his clan, he moved the administrative capital to Edo (modern Tokyo), leaving the more or less impotent imperial court behind at Kyoto. At Edo he built the enormous impregnable fortress which, after the Meiji Restoration two and a half centuries later, was to become the Imperial Palace.

In order to forestall any *coup d'état*, Ieyasu forced the daimio to spend a large part of their time at Edo and, when living in their provincial domains, to leave their wives and families at Edo as hostages. As a further precaution he created a force of secret police to ferret out potential conspirators against the regime, thus acquiring the dubious distinction of creating the world's first police state.

Whereas Hideyoshi had for a time tolerated proselytizing by the early Portuguese and Spanish missionaries, Ieyasu considered them to be dangerous outriders of a foreign sovereign, the Pope of Rome. As such, he exiled them from Japan while permitting the Dutch Protestants, who were traders rather than missionaries, to maintain a limited trading post near Nagasaki. (In 1637 a rebellion of Christian converts in Kyushu was ruthlessly repressed, but the strength of this uprising frightened the Tokugawa government and caused it to take drastic measures against any sort of foreign influence.)

Not only were foreign ships henceforth forbidden to enter Japanese ports but also Japanese merchants were forbidden to sail to foreign countries and the building of ocean-going vessels was prohibited. Overseas Japanese, like those who had settled in Manila, were not permitted to return. As a result the once profitable Japanese foreign trade languished and Japan entered upon a prolonged period of self-isolation which postponed for over 250 years its emergence as a major power in Asia.

Tokugawa Japan*

The Tokugawa period (1600–1868) was one of rigid centralized control during which the Japanese people became a docile herd, watched by secret police and indoctrinated with a revived Confucianism that taught politeness and obedience to samurai, the intellectuals and scholars, the peasants and, lowest of all, the merchants and manufacturers. Priests instilled a martial spirit in the warrior class whose members adopted a strict code of knightly behavior involving suicide by hara-kiri in the event of disgrace or defeat and a contemptuous aloofness from money-making or menial work. In effect, the Tokugawa shogunate preserved internal peace by imposing a feudal structure and mentality which was already outdated in Europe and had not existed in China for almost one thousand years.

Nevertheless, in spite of the imposition of an anachronistic social and economic order, the prolonged internal peace brought with it an unprecedented prosperity. Although the merchant class was placed at the bottom of the social scale, it grew and thrived, at first by controlling the rice crop and then by creating domestic industry. A genuine capitalist class emerged into which many of the increasingly impoverished samurai married. The cities grew and came to dominate the Tokugawa economy which, in theory, was still based upon agriculture. Under the patronage of wealthy city dwellers, the

---

* Japan's Tokugawa period almost exactly covers the time between the founding of the British colonies in North America and the firm establishment of the unity of the United States after the Civil War.

arts flourished, in large measure as amusement for "tired businessmen." (So also did the brothels and inns which lined the Tokaido Highway between Edo and Kyoto.) Artists and writers, instead of catering to the imperial court or the feudal aristocracy, began to produce popular poems, block prints and Kabuki plays which stressed realism. Within the antiquated feudal order, a bourgeois society rapidly developed, dominated by a few great merchant families. These were the forerunners of the later Zaibatsu combines, organized by the Mitsuis, the Mitsubishis and the Sumitomos.

Under Ieyasu, a new floridly ornate style of Japanese architecture developed, contrasting with the ascetic simplicity of the earlier buildings at Nara and Kyoto. At the nation's capital, Ieyasu built himself Nijo Castle, elaborately decorated in gold and equipped with "nightingale floors" whose squeaking would warn of the approach of an assassin. Other examples of this Momoyama style soon appeared in various parts of Japan. The period culminated in the erection by Ieyasu's grandson of the great Toshogu Shrine at Nikko, dedicated to his grandfather. This monumental temple combined Shinto symbols with Chinese Buddhist features reminiscent of the Nara period. It was paid for by a forced levy upon the daimio and took 15,000 artisans three years to build.

Ieyasu has remained the outstanding symbol of Japan's seventeenth and eighteenth centuries.

The isolation from the outside world enforced by the Tokugawa produced a strong spirit of nationalism and a sense of superiority; both were deliberately fostered by a renascence of Shinto worship that emphasized the individuality of Japanese culture and the divine origin of the emperor.

Secure in their control of the country, the later Tokugawa shoguns eventually began to permit the importation of European (mostly Dutch) books and to encourage the study of Western developments even while still rigorously excluding foreign visitors.

By the middle of the nineteenth century, after more than 250 years of internal peace under the Tokugawa, Japan had in many respects become a modern nation-state despite its technological backwardness and its outdated feudal structure of society.

Neither India nor China enjoyed a comparable period of peace during the seventeenth and eighteenth centuries.

Mogul India

In 1526 the Afghan Babar descended upon and conquered India, founding the Mogul dynasty which was to rule India until it gradually fell under British rule. Akbar, the greatest of the Mogul emperors, ruled from 1556 to 1605, reuniting the warring states of northern India and extending his rule over Bengal and the southern Dravidian states. (The height of Mogul power corresponded roughly to the reign of Queen Elizabeth in England and the first English settlement in North America.) Shortly after Akbar's death, Mogul power began to decline as India fell more and more under European domination. Akbar himself may have been partly responsible for European intrusion because he exhibited an even greater tolerance toward foreigners than the Ming emperors of China. Refusing to permit any form of religious discrimination, Akbar encouraged public debate on all subjects and idealistically attempted to establish a religious faith and morality based upon what seemed to him noblest and most humane in all the known creeds. With his sincere belief in the brotherhood of man, Akbar came closer than the contemporary followers of Jesus to realizing the professed principles of Christianity.

Under Akbar's son, Jahangir, the arts flourished, especially painting; and under his grandson, Shah Jahan (1628–1658), came the climax of Mogul splendor; Shah Jahan built the famous Peacock Throne and the Taj Mahal, as well as the Pearl Mosque in Agra, but beneath all the magnificence there was decay, with poverty and misery among the people. Shah Jahan was intolerant in religious matters and ruled as a cruel despot. Akbar's toleration and good government were things of the past. The last of the great Mogul emperors was Aurangzeb, who reigned from 1659 to 1707—an austere puritan and bigot who destroyed Hindu temples and persecuted followers of the Hindu religion. After his death the decaying empire was ripe for foreign conquest.

The Portuguese had received friendly treatment from Akbar, although their settlement at Goa was a thorn in his side. During the reign of Jahangir the English appeared on the scene. In 1615 Sir Thomas Roe, an ambassador sent by James I, obtained concessions which laid the foundation of the East India Company's trade. An English fleet defeated the Portuguese in Indian waters. In 1629 there was war between Shah Jahan and the Portuguese. Portugal's star was fading. By 1641 the English and the Dutch had all but driven Portugal out of the East. The English established trading posts near Madras and Surat, and founded the city of Madras in 1639. The Dutch took over Ceylon and the East Indies. In 1662 Charles II of England married Catharine of Braganza and received the island of Bombay as a dowry, which he sold for almost nothing to the East India Company. In 1690 the Englishman Job Charnok founded the city of Calcutta. And now the French entered upon the scene, founding a post at

Surat in 1668 and acquiring by purchase the city of Pondicherry, which soon became the most important part of the east coast.

During the century that followed Aurangzeb's death in 1707, India was in turmoil—an ideal state for plunderers and adventurers. England and France, at war with each other in Europe, competed for the spoils in India, alternately fighting and seducing the disunited native provincial rulers. Among the latter were the Marathas, the Sikhs, the Rajputs and a number of princelings. For a time the Marathas in central India seemed to have inherited the Mogul empire, but their power soon faded. Whenever there was a dispute among the native rulers, the English would back one side and the French the other, always taking what advantage they could for themselves. After fifteen years of struggle (1746–1761), the English won, with Robert Clive, the empire-builder, triumphant over his French rival, Dupleix. Not only had Britain achieved mastery of the seas but Clive had the backing of the East India Company and the British Parliament, while behind Dupleix there stood only the weak government of Louis XV. The Battle of Plassey, in 1759, at which Clive tricked and defeated the native Nawab of Bengal and his French aides, established British control of eastern India and laid the foundation for an empire that would eventually comprise the whole subcontinent, as well as Ceylon. (Ceylon was taken from the Portuguese by the Dutch in 1660, and by the British from the Dutch in 1796.) But, before this empire could be established, there would be a century of divide-and-conquer policy—a century of intrigue, brutality, shameless exploitation and wars, culminating in the armed suppression of a great rebellion, known as the Sepoy Mutiny, in 1857.

Clive was a brigand of great skill and courage. His most shameful deed was the collection of full revenue in 1770, at a time when a great famine had wiped out one-third of the population of Bengal. Clive's successor, Warren Hastings, was hardly more scrupulous, although he liked Indians and robbed them not to enrich himself but for the benefit of the East India Company. Cornwallis, who came to rule in 1789, ended the most disreputable phase of early British rule, establishing a well-paid and well-trained civil service. As Sir Thomas Monro was later to put it, Cornwallis "purchased the integrity of the Company's servants by raising their allowances." Greater integrity did not, however, mean better treatment of the natives. In 1817 Monro, then Governor of Madras, wrote that, while other conquerors had been violent and cruel, "none has treated the natives with such scorn as we." * It was this scorn, openly expressed, that alienated the people of India more than exploitative-British rule. Not only the impoverished masses, but native rulers, many of them English-educated, were subjected to the same haughty treatment; and this was why the Sepoy† Mutiny became almost a national rebellion. After 1857 the British government took over rule from the East India Company and changed the policy to one of cooperation with the native princes, showing them respect provided that they were willing to act as puppets of the British raj. The result was that India showed remarkable loyalty toward Britain in World War I, in spite of the continued oppression of the masses. But this is getting ahead of our story.

* Quoted in N. H. Brailsford, *Subject India* (John Day, New York, 1943), pp. 9–10.

† Sepoy (*sipahi* in Hindustani): an Indian employed as a soldier by European powers.

China Under Manchu Rule

During the early years of the seventeenth century the Ming dynasty weakened and became unable to hold back the growing pressure of the Manchus in the northeast. Disorder spread, with bandit forces defying the central government and pirates ravaging the China coast. In 1644 the last of the Ming emperors committed suicide and the Manchu Ch'ing dynasty installed itself at Peking. Once again China fell under non-Chinese rule, and the people were ordered to wear their hair in queues as a sign of subservience, but the Confucian Mandarin bureaucracy retained its power.

The Manchu dynasty established an elaborate system of courier relays by means of which orders from Peking could be transmitted with remarkable speed to every part of the realm. However, the execution of these orders continued to entail traditional delay, pending the exaction of "squeeze" by the local officials.

Under the Emperors Nurhachu, K'ang-Hsi and Chien Lung, there followed a period of relative stability and progress. Formosa was annexed in 1683 and a native revolt was suppressed in 1721. (A considerable number of Ming adherents had fled to Formosa, much as the Chinese Nationalists were to take refuge there more than two centuries later.) The Manchu rulers restored the empire's authority in central Asia and suppressed disorders in Tibet in 1717 and again in 1747. Chien Lung, the last of the three strong Manchu emperors, succeeded in temporarily stemming the rising tide of European intrusion by limiting foreigners to the use of a single Chinese port at Canton, but the menace of the "new imperialism" already was casting its shadow over the Celestial Realm. As the forces of Protestant evangelism joined with those of mercantile greed to demand entry into China, the Manchus, like the native Chinese emperors, refused to deal with the foreign powers as equals. Confucian China, weak though it had become, continued to view all non-Chinese nations and peoples as inferior, entitled at most to become tribute-paying vassals.

In 1792 King George III of England sent a mission to Peking under Lord Macartney, who was formally received by the Emperor Chien Lung. In declining to lift or alter the restrictions or foreign trade, the emperor wrote to King George:

> You, O King, live beyond the confines of many seas. Nevertheless, impelled by your humble desire to partake of the benefits of our civilization, you have despatched a mission respectfully bearing your memorial. . . . To show your devotion you have also sent offerings of your country's produce. I have read your memorial; the earnest terms in which it is cast reveal a respectful humility on your part which is highly praiseworthy. . . .
>
> Swaying the wide world, I have but one aim in view, namely to maintain a perfect governance and to fulfill the duties of the state. Strange and costly objects do not interest me. I have no use for your country's manufactures. It behooves you, O King, to respect my sentiments and to display even greater devotion and loyalty in future, so that by perpetual submission to our throne, you may secure peace and prosperity for your country hereafter. . . . Tremblingly obey and show no negligence.*

* Quoted by Jawaharlal Nehru in *Glimpses of World History* (John Day, New York, 1942), pp. 333–334.

3

The Rise of
Western Imperialism

The astonishing fact about the seventeenth and eighteenth centuries was that the chronically quarreling nations of western Europe were able to establish world empires during a period when their own countries were ravaged and their populations decimated by a series of religious and dynastic wars.

The Spaniards, no longer dominant on the Continent and almost continuously at war, managed to maintain and even to expand their American empire, imposing their rule and their religion upon peoples more numerous than those of Spain itself.

The Dutch, having thrown off Spanish rule, took over a declining Portugal's domination of the African coast, settled Cape Town, seized control of the fabulously rich East Indies, and, on the other side of the world, established settlements in and north of Brazil and in the West Indies, and even founded a short-lived settlement at New Amsterdam (New York).

Elizabethan England challenged Spain at sea, competed with the Dutch in displacing Portugal in Asia, founded colonies in North America and presently displaced the Dutch at New Amsterdam.

The France of Henry IV, while still recovering from the religious wars of the sixteenth century, was already reaching out to found settlements in the New World. By the middle of the seventeeth century, under the guidance of Cardinal Richelieu, adviser to Louis XIII, France had become a powerful nation and was challenging Austria and Spain for hegemony on the Continent.

The German states had not yet recovered from the devastation of the Thirty Years' War (1618–1648),* but Sweden established two settlements along the Middle Atlantic coast of North America, soon to be lost to the Dutch and English.

The French "Sun King," Louis XIV, dominated the European scene during his long reign (1638–1715) and engaged in a protracted dynastic struggle with the Hapsburgs. To prevent his conquest of the Continent, Britain and Holland joined Austria in a coalition and succeeded in halting French expansion at the turn of the century. The War of the Spanish Succession (1701–1714) ended in a nominal victory for France, but Britain was its main beneficiary. Under the Treaty of Utrecht a Bourbon king was installed in Spain but, while the land powers were locked in combat, Britain seized Minorca and Gibraltar from Spain and acquired Newfoundland, Acadia and the vast Hudson Bay territory from France. Having already displaced Portugal in the inhuman trade in African

---

* The Thirty Years' War began as a religious conflict between Protestants and Catholics, but developed into a political revolt of the Protestant German states against the Holy Roman Empire.

slaves, Britain now demanded and received from Spain the sole right to supply African slaves to the Spanish colonies in America. Under the Treaty of Utrecht, Spain was also forced to yield territory in the Netherlands to the Elector of Brandenburg, who promptly proclaimed himself King of Prussia.

As Prussia emerged as a major power on the Continent, Tsar Peter the Great brought Russia for the first time into the European picture. Defeating the Swedes and advancing his domains to the Baltic, Peter moved the Russian capital from Moscow to St. Petersburg.

In 1740 another war broke out, this time over the Austrian succession. Between 1740 and 1748, while England fought both France and Spain, Frederick the Great led Prussia to victory over Austria and took possession of Silesia.

Alarmed by the suddenly displayed military might of Prussia, Austria and France, hitherto fierce dynastic rivals, joined hands with each other and with the Empress Elizabeth of Russia to crush the Prussian upstart. Britain, ever careful to preserve a balance of power on the Continent, subsidized Frederick the Great, who, in the first three years of the Seven Years' War (1756–1763) successively defeated the French, the Austrians and the Russians. In 1759 Frederick suffered defeat by a combined Austrian-Russian army, but a year later came back to win a resounding victory over the Austrians at Liegnitz. Meanwhile the Russians seized Frederick's capital, Berlin. Things might have gone badly for "Old Fritz" had not the Russian empress died and been succeeded by Peter III, who promptly switched sides and thereby sealed Prussia's victory.

Once more Britain was the chief beneficiary of a struggle between the Continental powers. With her hands more or less freed by Frederick's campaigns, Britain was able to launch another attack upon the overseas possessions of both France and Spain. In what American history books call "the French and Indian Wars," the English and their American colonists seized Canada from France as well as all the lands lying between the British colonies and the Mississippi River. Florida was taken from Spain. Almost simultaneously, Britain drove France out of India. In 1763 Britain was established as the world's leading colonial power and as the unchallenged mistress of the seas. However, in little more than a decade Britain was to lose more than she had gained in America.

Oppressive taxation and ruthless mercantile exploitation by Britain of its thirteen North American colonies led to their revolt against the British crown. Substantially aided by France, the colonies defeated the forces sent to subdue them and, in 1783, established their independence as the United States of America.

The American Revolution was the first successful colonial revolt against any of the European powers. It was also the first successful assertion of the right of all peoples to self-determination and self-government—an event which shook the thrones of absolute monarchy throughout Europe.

In 1789 revolution broke out in France, resulting in the overthrow of the monarchy, the execution of Louis XVI and Marie Antoinette and the proclamation of a republic. However, the revolution was aborted when Napoleon Bonaparte became a virtual dictator under the five-man Directoire in 1789 and, three years later, assumed the title of Emperor of France.

There then followed the twelve well-known years of the Napoleonic Wars during which Napoleon spread turmoil throughout Europe, paradoxically fostering revolution while at the same time seeking to establish a world empire. Defeating a series of coalitions formed against him, the little Corsican conquered most of Europe as well as Egypt. In the end he was defeated by British sea power and a reckless invasion of the vast tsarist empire. (Trafalgar in 1805 destroyed the French and Spanish fleets. Thereafter the British blockade of the Continent whittled away Napoleon's power until he was ruined by his Russian adventure.) In 1813 Napoleon's empire collapsed. Paris fell in 1814 and the would-be world conqueror fled to Elba. Returning from there for the famous desperate last effort of the "Hundred Days," Napoleon met final defeat at the hands of Britain and Prussia in the Battle of Waterloo.

Britain, Prussia, Austria and Russia met at the Congress of Vienna in an endeavor to restore as much as they could of the antebellum status. A Bourbon was placed upon the throne at Paris and the Concert of Powers determined to protect Europe against further revolutionary ferment. But the flame had been kindled. It would take time, other wars and other revolutions to establish the rights of man in the Old World, but, in the New World of America, the Spanish colonies wasted little time in establishing their independence. To all intents and purposes, the European powers had now lost America—but they had not lost their lust for colonial empire.

Before we turn to the European invasion of the Far East, it is necessary to note the rapid growth of two great land empires, Russia and the United States.

Russian Overland Expansion

Russian eastward expansion began in the sixteenth century under Tsar Ivan "the Terrible" (reigned 1547–1584), who won Kazan and Astrakhan from the Tartar Mongols and pushed into Siberia, while simultaneously advancing his western frontier toward the coveted Baltic. Some of his gains were lost during a time of trouble under Tsars Feodor and Boris

Godunov, but expansion was resumed under Michael, the first of the Romanovs, who ruled from 1613 until 1646. In 1647 the Russians established a post on the Sea of Okhotsk which, although they did not know it, opened upon the Pacific Ocean. In 1741 Vitus Bering crossed the strait which bears his name and claimed Alaska and the Aleutian Islands. At the end of the eighteenth century, the dominion of the Tsars covered over seven million square miles, compared to the five million square miles of the Spanish empire at its height. Russia's population equaled that of France, then the most populous European nation. In fact, after his disastrous retreat from Russia in 1812, Napoleon expressed the view that some day Russia would rule the world.

Expansion of the United States

The westward expansion of the United States, like the Russian eastward drive, was favored by the fact that it progressed through sparsely inhabited territory; it was similarly hampered by the difficulties of overland transportation. However, North America possessed a far more favorable climate than central Asia and Siberia, and was far better endowed with natural resources. Moreover, unlike the illiterate Russian emigrants into Asia—many of them involuntary exiles—the Americans who moved toward the Pacific benefited from the industrial revolution, the building of railroads and the explosion of technological development that was taking place in the Atlantic area.

A vast tract of land west of the Mississippi was acquired by purchase from France in 1803 (the Louisiana Purchase). The Floridas were acquired in 1819. Wars against the Indians and broken treaties with them drove the unfortunate aborigines farther and farther westward in campaigns that wholly disregarded their rights. In 1848 a predatory war with Mexico, followed by a settlement with Britain of the northwestern frontier, completed the conquest of the North American continent south of the Canadian border. In 1867 Alaska was acquired by purchase from Russia for the paltry sum of seven million dollars. The United States had every reason to be satisfied with its territorial status.

In addition, by tacit agreement with Britain, the United States had declared under the Monroe Doctrine of 1823 that it would not tolerate any European interference in the newly-established independence of the Latin American republics.

With the entire Western Hemisphere under its control, except for British-owned Canada, one might have expected that the United States would have no interest in creating an overseas empire. Nevertheless, the United States was about to join the European powers in an invasion of the Far East.

The Western Intrusion into China

Having lost most of her American empire and with India substantially under control, Britain became increasingly insistent upon "opening up" the ancient Empire of China. Restricted to the use of a single Chinese port, Canton, by the Manchu rulers, British merchants endeavored to increase their trade by using opium grown in India to pay for their imports of tea, silk, porcelain and other marketable Chinese products. This involved a propagation of the deadly habit of opium-smoking by the Chinese. The Emperor Tao Kuang (1820–1850) quite naturally attempted to suppress this harmful traffic, but the British resorted to force to maintain it. The emperor resisted but, in the first "Opium War" fought in

1839–1842, his ill-armed Chinese forces were unable to defend themselves against Britain's superior power, and China, badly defeated, was forced to cede actual possession of Hong Kong to Britain, to open five additional ports to British trade, to accept the "most favored nation" clause in commercial treaties, and to pay an indemnity of twenty-one million dollars. France and the United States—the latter under its developing "me-too" (open-door) policy—quickly demanded and obtained similar commercial rights as well as an "extraterritorial" status for their citizens. Under these "unequal treaties," foreigners could not be tried in Chinese courts for either civil or criminal offenses committed on Chinese soil.

The reigns of the Manchu Emperors Hsien Feng and T'ung Chih were marked by internal trouble as well as by foreign intrusion. In 1796–1803 there had been a widespread revolt (the White Lotus Rebellion) expressing protest against the growing imbalance of China's population and food supply. The population had risen from about fifty million under the Ming dynasty to nearly three hundred million under the Manchus without a corresponding increase in agricultural production, due largely to the fact that territorial expansion under the Manchus had added mostly uncultivated land. The rebellion had been suppressed but, between 1850 and 1864, the far more serious Tai Ping revolt caused widespread devastation and disruption. The revolt was sparked by pseudo-Christian Chinese leaders who expressed not only traditional peasant grievances but also hostility to Manchu rule and foreign intrusion. Sensing that their own interests were threatened by the revolt against central authority, the foreign powers eventually aided in its suppression. Yet, in spite of this collusion with the Manchu regime, the relations between the foreign powers and Peking remained strained. Accustomed to deal with "barbarian" outsiders as inferiors, Peking resisted the establishment of diplomatic relations that would involve formal foreign representation at the capital. Anglo-French pressure for such representation mounted, not only to obtain further concessions but also to protect the growing number of Protestant and Catholic missionaries. Finally Britain's Lord Palmerston decided to seek an excuse to apply force. When a number of incidents supplied this excuse, the British and French launched an attack which ended the effective restoration of Manchu rule. The so-called Second Opium War ended with the Anglo-French capture of Peking, the imposition of another large indemnity and the opening of eleven more Chinese ports to foreign trade. Those parts of the China coast not already in foreign hands were ravaged by pirates, while, in the northwest and north, Russia was steadily pushing against the frontiers of the harassed Chinese Empire.

The Russians, hostile to Britain's colonial expansion, had not joined the European sea powers in their more or less cooperative maneuvering in China; they were playing a game of their own. The Manchu government, seeking a counterweight to Anglo-American-French pressures, accepted a Russian offer to mediate between itself and the importunate Westerners. As a reward for this mediation, Peking gave Russia title to the territory north of the Amur River and east of the Ussuri, where the Russians promptly built the city of Vladivostok.

Britain eyed these Russian gains with misgivings and, for a time, flirted with the idea of allying itself with China; but the growing weakness of the Manchu Empire presented an irresistible invitation to further aggrandizement at China's expense. While France was pushing her way into Annam, the British similarly flouted traditional Chinese suzerainty over Burma and asserted their control over that country.

As the Manchu Empire thus tottered toward its fall, a new hungry competitor in its dismemberment was arising across the China Sea. Japan had not escaped the rising tide of Western intrusion, but its ultimate fate was destined to be quite different from that of the unhappy Celestial Kingdom.

Japan Pried Open

Early in the nineteenth century, Yankee traders had developed an interest in the Far East, sending their clipper ships around the Horn into the China Sea. As steamships began to supplant sailing vessels, coaling stations suddenly became important. Japan, hitherto rigidly closed to foreigners under the Tokugawa regime, seemed to the American government an ideal location for such facilities. In 1853 Commodore Matthew Perry had arrived with four American warships off the Edo coast and presented to the shogun's representative a letter from the American President, demanding the opening of Japanese ports and the negotiation of a trade treaty.

The demand caused consternation at Edo. Realizing that Japan would be unable to defend itself against the powerful guns of the American "black ships," the shogun decided to do what no shogun had done for 600 years—to consult the emperor at Kyoto. Perry had retired to the Ryukyu Islands and announced that he would return in the following spring for an answer. The people at both Edo and Kyoto were divided in their opinions. The older daimio and especially the powerful lords of Satsuma and Choshu were in favor of rejecting the demand. The younger and more realistic samurai and some of the elders at Edo and at the imperial court recognized the helplessness of their country and favored acceptance of the inevitable, hoping to use the unwanted presence of the foreigners to acquire the knowledge and means to equip their country for modern warfare. When Perry returned, no decision had been reached. It was not until 1864 that the bombardment of the Choshu coast by an Anglo-French fleet convinced even the conservatives that resistance to the Western powers would be futile. Nevertheless, when the shogun agreed in 1867 to the American demand for a trade treaty, a revolt against the Tokugawa regime spread rapidly throughout the land.

The Tokugawa shogunate had for years been losing its vigor. Almost its sole solid support came from the feudal lords, whose privilege and power derived from Edo. At first the revolt combined a demand for the restoration of the power of the emperor with violent anti-Westernism and the expectation that he would throw out the foreigners. Very soon, however, the rebellious feudal lords dropped their demand for the expulsion of foreigners and concentrated upon the abolition of the shogunate. For a time a disastrous civil war seemed inevitable. When the last Tokugawa shogun resigned after agreeing to an American trade treaty, some of his feudal adherents refused to accept the end of the shogunate. On January 28, 1868, these last die-hards were defeated at the battle of Toba by the forces supporting the emperor's restoration.

Meanwhile, no sooner had the trade treaty with the United States been signed than England, France and Russia demanded and obtained similar concessions. Five Japanese ports were opened to foreign trade and the little fishing village of Yokohama quickly became a thriving center of foreign commerce.

The Meiji Restoration

January 3, 1868, marked the resumption of imperial rule by the fifteen-year-old Emperor Meiji. A few months later the court left Kyoto and established Edo, now renamed Tokyo (meaning Eastern Capital), as the seat of imperial government. In the following year the daimio fiefs were abolished and the feudal lords became prefectural governors of their formerly independent domains. The series of dramatic moves which followed were undertaken by the young emperor upon the advice of a remarkable group of younger samurai and a few elder statesmen. These measures included the sending of study missions to Europe and the United States; the inauguration of a mail service; the installation of a railroad and a telegraph line between Tokyo and Yokohama; the establishment of a ministry of education; the adoption of universal military service; the institution of a new land-tax system; and the lifting of the ban upon Christianity. All these reforms were undertaken between 1868 and 1873.

In 1874 a Japanese military expedition to Formosa forced China to pay an indemnity for a Formosan attack upon Ryukyu merchants. In the following years, treaties were signed with Russia and Korea.* A small, new, modern navy was constructed at Satsuma. The army was reorganized on Prussian lines, previous French influence having waned after the French defeat at the hands of Germany in 1871. With the creation of a peasant army, the samurai were forbidden to carry swords and their hereditary pensions were ended by reasonably generous lump-sum payments. Many of the warrior-knights became officers in the new army; others became businessmen. Almost overnight Japan converted itself from its feudal state into modern nationhood.

The reform was far-reaching. In 1881 the Emperor Meiji issued a decree promising the creation of a popularly elected

---

* In 1866 the French Asiatic squadron under Admiral Roze had attempted to open up the "hermit kingdom" of Korea. The attempt was unsuccessful. Five years later an attempt by United States Rear Admiral Rogers to duplicate Perry's success in Japan likewise failed. Korea remained closed to foreigners until, in 1867, it signed a trade treaty with Japan.

national assembly. Political parties were founded. Missions were sent abroad to study constitutional forms. In 1889 a constitution was adopted and General Yamagata became the first premier. A year later the first Diet was elected. For the first time in its history Japan became, or at least started to become, a country ruled by its people.

Not all the supporters of the Meiji Restoration were happy with the reforms instituted by the new regime. A conservative revolt in Satsuma had been forcibly repressed in 1877. Generals and admirals were already beginning to show a reluctance to submit to civilian authority, although this was not yet apparent to an outsider.

Unlike the Chinese, the people of Japan showed themselves capable of coming to terms with the modern world. Like accomplished practitioners of judo, they used the impact of foreign incursion to give momentum to their own long-delayed revolution, borrowing whatever seemed useful and suitable to them from the foreigners who had forced open their doors. (Had the Tai P'ing Rebellion not been aborted, something similar might have happened in China to save the empire from final disaster, but the Chinese were too self-sufficient and too convinced of their cultural superiority to learn from the despised Western "barbarians." The Japanese had the great advantage of having lived for centuries next to a Chinese neighbor whom they recognized as physically and culturally superior, and from whom they were accustomed to borrow. China, considering itself the center of an unmatched civilization, proved itself incapable of using the intrusion of the rapacious West to reform its outdated and corrupt Confucian organization.)

Despite the anachronistic structure of Japanese society during the long Tokugawa period, the rise of a bourgeois middle class had prepared the nation's economy and its spirit for an incredibly rapid adaptation to modern technology and political organization. The danger to Japan's future lay in the fact that the shogunate had also nurtured an arrogant nationalism, ready to employ modernization in adventures of military conquest. In this respect, the Western powers, from which Japan was learning much that was good, had set and were setting a truly horrendous example.

The world into which Japan emerged was a world dominated by the "new imperialism." Britain was the world's leading imperial power; it had started the industrial revolution and now excelled all its rivals in industrial development. It possessed the world's most powerful navy and owned almost one-half of the world's mercantile tonnage. This was the heyday of Kipling's Victorian England; Britannia not only ruled the waves but "an empire upon which the sun never set."

Pax Britannica?

The century between Waterloo and Sarajevo is often referred to as the era of the *Pax Britannica*. It could be more appropriately described as a century of British conquest. To be sure, the major western European powers temporarily ceased warring among each other after Bismarck's victories over Austria, Denmark and France between 1866 and 1871. But, during the *Pax Britannica*, almost every year was marked by relatively minor wars in most of which Britain was directly or indirectly involved.

In Europe the waning power of the Turkish Empire created a growing vacuum into which Russia threatened to expand. Britain and France halted this threat by defeating Russia in the Crimean War of 1853–1856. Then, in 1877, Russia defeated the Turks and, as the Turks retreated from the Balkans, Russia and Austria-Hungary each sought to gain influence in this area.

In expanding their Asian empire, the British fought the two Opium Wars against China and five major wars in India, including the suppression of the Sepoy Mutiny in 1857.

By 1900 all of Africa, excepting only Liberia and Ethiopia, had been carved up into colonial possessions by the European powers. Under the protection of their alliance with Britain, the Portuguese had retained possession of Angola and Mozambique. In 1807 the British had seized Cape Town from the Dutch settlers, who moved northward in "the Long Trek" to Transvaal and Natal only to be conquered by the British in the Boer War of 1899–1900 and to have their fabulously rich country become a British dominion. After the Suez Canal was opened in 1869, Britain occupied Egypt to protect her new "life line to India." Between 1884 and 1900, the British gained possession of the Sudan, British East Africa (later Kenya and the Rhodesias) and part of Somaliland, while, on the west coast, they annexed Nigeria, Sierra Leone and the Gold Coast (now Ghana).

Meanwhile France had conquered and annexed Algeria, Tunis and part of Somaliland, established protectorates over Madagascar and the French Congo, and gained control over the greater part of the Sahara Desert. The Belgian Congo, at first a ruthlessly exploited personal possession of King Leopold I of Belgium, became a Belgian colony. Spain claimed parts of Morocco and Guinea and held possession of Rio de Oro. Germany, a late entry into the race for colonial empire, had acquired Kamerun, a large slice of Southwest Africa and another in Southeast Africa.

79

The boundaries of these European acquisitions of African territory bore little or no relation to the original tribal, linguistic or cultural frontiers.

Let us now see how this world of 1893 impressed a young German globe-trotter. His own country had already grabbed its share of Africa, but it had not yet muscled its way into the game of carving up China. There is no indication in my father Paul Warburg's diary that he was aware of his own country's imminent challenge to Britain's world supremacy. Much less did he dream that his beloved Japan was at the very point of embarking upon a career of conquest or that the remote United States, soon to become the country of his adoption, stood poised at the brink of imperialist adventure in Asia.

4

Excerpts from a Globe-Trotter's Diary (1892-1893)

In December 1892 my father and two young German friends set out from Hamburg on a trip around the world. Journeying by rail to Genoa, they boarded the North German Lloyd steamer *Hohenstaufen* en route from Bremen to Australia. The *Hohenstaufen* was not much of a ship; in order to steady her in a storm, her captain hoisted sail; the vessel carried a deckload of "six oxen, four calves and assorted chickens, ducks and geese," presumably to be eaten by an English family bound for Australia.

Halfway through the Suez Canal, at Ismailia, the three young travelers debarked in order to spend a week in Egypt. Thence they boarded an English ship to Aden, where they transferred to another English vessel bound for Bombay. From there they proceeded overland across India to Delhi, Agra, Patna and Calcutta and, from there, by ship to Madras and Ceylon. A French vessel took them from Colombo to Singapore and Saigon and, eventually, to Hong Kong. After brief visits to Canton, Macao and Shanghai, they crossed the China Sea to Japan, where they spent a month before returning home to Germany via Canada and the United States.

Japan was clearly the magnet which drew my father to Asia, perhaps because it was a country as yet little explored by Europeans. In 1893, only thirty-nine years had elapsed since Japan's tightly locked doors had been forced open. The last of the Tokugawa shoguns was still living—an old gentleman in retirement at Ejiri.

It also seems likely that Germans—particularly, young Germans—may at this time have felt a certain affinity for Dai Nippon. Both nations had emerged upon the world scene at almost exactly the same time; the Meiji Restoration had taken place in 1868; Germany had been welded together in Bismarck's "blood and iron" in 1871. Both peoples had a long history of military prowess. Both were orderly, disciplined, industrious and obedient to higher authority. The Prussian army had served as a model for the modernization of Japan's armed forces and Bismarck's new constitution for the Reich had been carefully studied and in part imitated by the Japanese. Finally, both countries had a strong feudal tradition, extending back to the Teutonic knights and the samurai.

I am inclined to think, however, that Japan's attraction for my father was largely aesthetic. I think it likely that he had seen some Japanese works of art, bits of handicraft or photographs brought back to Hamburg by one or more of the merchant-traders who were clients of the Warburg banking house, and that he had become fascinated by the landscape, the architecture and the costumes of this distant, mysterious land. This seems to me plausible because my father's taste ran to simplicity, to line rather than to color, and to miniature perfection rather than to grandiose concept. From this point of view, Japan was made to order for him.

Throughout his journey, at least up to the end of his visit to Japan, my father wrote daily and often long letters to his parents in Hamburg. He wrote with a pencil and kept carbon copies. Some time ago I translated these yellowed, closely written pages of German script for the benefit of my family. A few excerpts are presented in this chapter. (Unfortunately my father either stopped writing after he left Japan or else his letters concerning his journey homeward, via Canada and the United States, have been lost.)

About Ancient and Modern Egypt

"The ancient Egyptians were keen observers of nature. The eternal cycle of birth and death had an important place in their religion. They were far more aware than we of their allotted life span. Looking back upon their amazing culture, one is tempted to think that the pyramids, those great mausoleums, were erected half in mockery of future generations. They seem to cry out: 'Look! This is what *we* were able to do! Read our hieroglyphics, if you can! They spell out our accomplishments. Use your short stay on earth to show what *you* can do!' Alas, later generations have plundered the ancient monuments and even used some of them as stone quarries!

"Everything about the Egypt-that-was is indescribably impressive; not so the life of the present-day inhabitants. For the past week I have been unable to escape a feeling of utter disgust as I observed the way of life of these subhumans.

"One feels sympathy for any upward-striving people, considering any unpleasant conditions as at least improvements over an even more unpleasant past. But, in the case of a decadent civilization such as this, the present low level of life is

83

only a promise of further decay. These people are filthy, lazy and apathetic. They sit on the curbstone or flat on the sidewalk in front of a café and smoke, when they are not begging. They let their animals and the fertile soil do their 'work' for them and yet they show a cruelty toward their donkeys, camels and horses such as one seldom sees anywhere. Handwork is done only when absolutely necessary, and then badly. This is evidenced by their houses of half-baked clay and in the faulty use of materials. In their mosques one sees columns of varying heights, used simply because they were easily available. When these people work at all, they act as if they were suffering martyrdom, moving overhastily, assuming the most awkward positions and using the wrong tools. Most of the heavy work is done by women and children while the men loll about. . . .

"Pottery costs next to nothing and is easy to make, yet they collect their water in old petroleum tins. The custodian of a mosque did his 'cleaning' in the following way: he filled a small, dirty tin can with water out of the inevitable petroleum tin, filled his mouth with the water and blew it, like a human atomizer, on the floor, which he then swept carelessly with an ineffective broom made of palm leaves. . . .

"Wheeled vehicles are rarely used. The Egyptians overload their donkeys and camels and then add their own weight to the load. . . . The men consider themselves the lords of the universe and enjoy wholly undeserved privileges over the women. The latter, in their black veils, run about like muzzled and beaten dogs. . . .

"Nevertheless, I would encourage anyone to visit Egypt. The ancient remains alone are worth the journey; and Moslem 'culture' is interesting for anyone who can bring himself to look at human beings as one looks at animals in a zoo."

En Route to Aden

"*Parametta* is an excellent ship. Its English crew and stewards are most efficient. Last night we passed Suez and are now steaming down the Red Sea with Mount Sinai to our left. . . . Passengers are not very interesting . . . several uncultured [*sic*] American tourists. . . . The English spend the whole day playing various deck games; at night they play whist . . . queer people.

"The Gaikwar of Baroda is on board, an Indian potentate with an annual income of several millions. He and his wife have a special table, together with their retinue, but his economic adviser dines alone; being a Brahman of a higher caste than the Gaikwar, he cannot eat at the same table. His Highness always precedes his wife and does not seem to speak to her very much. She is quite charming, especially when she shows her pretty teeth . . . in fact, she is the most attractive person on board. . . ."

At Aden, white and clean against green mountains topped by British forts and signal stations, a number of ships were riding at anchor, among them an Austrian cruiser bearing the ill-fated Archduke Franz Ferdinand, and the British liner *Oriental* which was to take on the *Parametta's* India-bound passengers.

Bombay

"A magnificent harbor full of white warships, among them the German *Schwalbe*. . . . Countless little boats swarm around our ship. One brings aboard a colorful group of admirers to welcome the Gaikwar; they hang wreaths around the necks of Their Highnesses. The Gaikwar, in his European clothes except for his turban, made a strange contrast with his white-clad subjects, who seemed sincerely glad to welcome him home. . . . We were among the first to be taken ashore in a small steamer and so were able to witness the Gaikwar's return to his native land. Two carriages, each with four horses, were waiting. Her Highness was carried in a palanquin into the first closed carriage; the Gaikwar mounted into the second open and flower-bedecked coach, and, amid wild hurrahs, the procession moved off with military precision on its way to the palace. Farewell, Gaikwar! And farewell, poor little lady, who must now return to the miserable lot of an Oriental wife! . . .

"Watson's Esplanade Hotel is overcrowded and not especially good. An incredible number of 'boys' are on hand to render various services . . . in a nearby park, Englishmen are playing cricket and tennis. . . .

"I like the people. They seem quiet, industrious and not without dignity. The men look strong, although a little thin in the legs. The women, unlike the Egyptians, do not wear veils; in their tasteful draperies, their erect carriage gives them a classical look, especially when carrying things on their heads.

"The Parsees, said to be descendants of the Persians, form the largest single group in Bombay's population. There are over 100,000 of them, easily identified by their black hats and their Semitic features. The Parsees are Zoroastrians, worshiping air, earth, water and fire. Their religion calls for 'good thoughts, good words and good deeds.' Unlike the Hindus, they consider all men equal.

"Bullocks are the beasts of burden in India and bullock carts the chief means of local transport. Donkeys are not mistreated as they are in Egypt. In fact, it is a pleasure to see the way Indians treat their animals."

India puzzled my father, not only because of the extreme contrasts in wealth and poverty, but because of its different layers of superimposed civilizations. Most of all, he seemed puzzled by the ambiguous relationships between the British raj and the Indian princes, and between the British and the multilingual, multiracial population of the vast subcontinent. The English he described, on the one hand, as "good colonizers who look after the welfare of their subjects," and, on the other hand, as "haughty and often brutal." They are "technically most efficient" but "curiously unable to agree upon a uniform gauge for the excellent railways they build." He remarked that "most Englishmen live in private houses or exclusive clubs; for foreigners they build the most enormous and outwardly elegant hotels in which the native servants are thieves, the food miserable, and the sheets, pillowcases, towels and napkins dirty and torn."

The following somewhat purple passage, written as his ship lay in the Hoogly River off Calcutta, perhaps best summarized my father's feelings:

"Farewell, India! Land of castes and philosophers! Land of the Himalayas and the tropical jungles! Land of repugnant liars and of beautiful people with sad eyes and compressed lips! Land of the moguls and maharajahs, farewell!

"Chew your betel-nut if you like but cast off your outdated religious frippery and superstition! Adopt the philosophy of your pandits and the practical sense of the English and then you will amount to something! Away with castes and child marriages! The Bengalis in Calcutta and the Parsees in Bombay are already headed in the right direction.

"And, as for you, my honorable English friends, get rid of the habit of beating and kicking your subject people before it is too late and try to achieve an understanding of them—oth-

87

erwise there will be another 1857 [the year of the Sepoy Mutiny]."

Ceylon

In Colombo my father had his first ride in a ricksha: " . . . a curious and not altogether comfortable feeling to be pulled by a man, as if he were an animal." However, he soon got used to this mode of travel, never ceasing to be amazed at the endurance and strong lungs of the sweating coolies.

There were many German planters and traders in Ceylon, to some of whom my father had letters of introduction. He dined at their houses, visited tea and cocoa plantations and a number of tropical gardens.

The French steamship *Natal* took the three globe-trotters from Colombo across to the coast of Sumatra and through the Strait of Malacca to Singapore.

"This morning at breakfast one of the Englishmen looked at the menu and asked for *'oeufs au choix.'* When the French steward asked what kind of eggs he wanted, he repeated firmly, pointing at the menu, *'oeufs au choix'* until I finally explained to him what *'au choix'* meant. Why do the English seem to think that if they repeat an order often enough and loudly enough, it will be understood?"

Saigon

"Four and a half hours of slowly steaming up the winding narrow river through flat, uninteresting, mosquito-infested country was not an alluring introduction to French Indochina. A few miles below Saigon we let off a shot from an ancient cannon to advise the *Messagerie Maritime* and the post office that we were coming. . . . I happened to call upon the French captain just as he was taking the picture of a pretty woman off the wall of his cabin and replacing it with a picture of his wife and children—undoubtedly for the benefit of the French authorities who would soon be coming on board! . . .

"The usual harbor scene. White-clad, pith-helmeted French officials, pigtailed stevedores and swarming little boats . . . upstream, an old troop ship and a few French gunboats. . . .

"Saigon consists of a post office, a rather decent cathedral and a few café-lined streets with French names. Except for the palms, the heat and the fact that drinks are served *sous la direction de Madame* by Chinese servants, one might think one is in Paris. Apart from the miserable Chinese quarter, Saigon is little more than the headquarters of *l'Armée Française de l'Indochine*. . . ."

In 1893 rubber planting was still in its infancy in Annam (South Vietnam) and the French were not yet firmly established in Tonkin (North Vietnam). In any case, Saigon had obviously not yet become a cosmopolitan center of trade, vice and graft. As my father saw it, Saigon must have been something like New Orleans in the early days of the nineteenth century.

"We have taken aboard a group of very dirty Chinese. They sit on the forward deck all morning, eating rice with their chopsticks or doing the opposite—in either case, fouling both the view and the atmosphere." (My father seems to have taken a dislike to the Chinese even before he reached China. He was perhaps overconscious of filth because Hamburg had quite recently suffered a severe epidemic of cholera.)

China

Upon arriving at Hong Kong: "A beautiful landfall. The early fog lifted and we could see the many green islands and, finally, the winding entrance to the harbor. Huge buildings line the shore—the British-looking town hall, several banks and a four-story hotel. The city seems to have climbed from the shore almost to the top of the Peak. In the harbor, merchant vessels and warships of many lands . . . As we have on board the commander of the Far East squadron of the Russian Imperial Navy, all sorts of neat little boats bring visitors to this important personage. . . . A colorful picture in which Chinese junks and sampans provide the background. On these man and wife row together, the wife frequently with a child on her back. . . . The captain maneuvered about in the harbor for two and a half hours—Lord knows why—before he finally dropped anchor. . . .

"As soon as we got ashore, I went to the Hong Kong-Shanghai Bank, where I was happy to find several letters. . . . Then a visit to Siemssen & Co. [probably a client of M. M. Warburg & Co. in Hamburg] and then tiffin at the hotel. After lunch, we looked at the town hall and then took a ricksha ride through the native quarter . . . narrow, steeply rising streets with vertical signs hanging in front of almost every house . . . bamboo poles on every floor with blue, black and white clothes hung out to dry. . . . The Chinese seem to like to carry loads, usually on a bamboo yoke with baskets or pails hung at each end. . . . Women clean the streets. . . . The picture lacks color, all the houses are the same, all the people wear the same clothes—grayish blue or black. . . .

"For those who can afford it and do not like climbing up or down the steep streets, the palanquin is the usual conveyance;

90

this is a wicker chair suspended from a bamboo pole shouldered at each end by a sweating coolie. They walk or trot tire-
lessly, always in step and at amazing speed, their heads covered by round, flat straw hats and their pigtails swinging from
side to side. . . .

"Service of meals at the hotel is peculiar. Each guest has a
blue-clad 'boy' behind his chair whose pigtail hangs down to
the floor. They hand you the menu, which is in Chinese with
the dishes numbered, and you point at whatever numbers
strike your fancy. I was lucky and got fish and boiled potatoes.

"We attended a play at a Chinese theater . . . it lasts
twenty-four hours, but we left after an hour and a half. . . .
Women's roles are played very well by men . . . of course,
we understood nothing except the slapstick comedy. . . .

"The English have built a funicular tramway to the top of
the Peak. The view from there is magnificent . . . blue,
island-dotted sea on three sides and, across the harbor, the
high, yellow-green mountains of the 'Middle Kingdom.' "

(In 1893, Kowloon had not yet been developed as an important part of the British Crown Colony, and the New Territories—some 350 square miles on the mainland—had not yet
been acquired under lease from China.)

Canton

March 11, 1893: "At 8 a.m. we set out for Canton on the
Hankow, a big American-style paddlewheeler. After three
hours we reached the mouth of the Sikiang (Pearl River)
. . . swampy fields of rice on either side with here and there
a rise of ground upon which the Emperor of the Middle Kingdom has set ramparts and cannon . . . at frequent intervals

the river is blocked by chains except for a narrow passage and this is protected by numerous Chinese gunboats and warships. . . .

"The nearer we come to Canton, the more frequent the settlements, topped by pagodas, and the livelier the river. . . . Gunboats, sailing junks loaded with goods for or from Hong Kong, small rowboats, boats with paddle wheels driven by the foot power of ten to twenty people, all swarming with human beings until, as we get to Canton, there seems scarcely an open spot on the river. Along the shore, rows of small craft in which 300,000 people are said to live . . . Canton lies on both sides of the river, a sea of roofs with the foreground concealed by houses on stilts, ships and a multitude of humanity. Incongruously, the scene on the north side of the river is dominated by a Christian cathedral.

"While our ship is still in midstream, some Chinese work their little boat up against the wheel box and jump headfirst through an open porthole; these are the baggage porters. Fifty feet from the dock we see our guide, Ah Bum, ordered for us by friends in Hong Kong, and in no time we are ashore and our baggage has been given into the hands of Schusan, a middle-aged, cross-eyed Chinese woman brought along by Ah Bum.

"In the palanquins which Ah Bum has ordered for us we proceed first of all to Shamien, the European settlement. A short distance through streets no wider than six feet brings us to the canal which surrounds the little island. Since the last uprising, the bridges over the canal have iron gates manned by watchmen. I doubt whether their ancient guns and spears would provide much protection, especially as the masses of available small boats could transport the Chinese across the canal all the way around the island.

"The settlement consists of about one hundred Europeans

who have made the most of their little island . . . clean gas-lit streets and neat houses, the club and a small church. . . . We were pleasantly received at a miniature hotel. I visited Mr. Bose [the German consul?] and then we set off on our wanderings. . . .

"What we saw of Canton in two days was more interesting than anything we have yet seen on our journey. Canton's streets are between four and seven feet in width. There are no horses or wagons. Nothing moves on wheels; everything is carried: and this is perhaps the most characteristic thing about the street scene.

"We are carried in three palanquins, each of us suspended from a bamboo pole upheld by three coolies. . . . They shout and push their way through an incredible mass of human beings. (There are said to be three million inhabitants.) For one who is used to more space, it seems impossible to move, but the people do move, pushing past each other and shouting. . . .

"On each side of the street there is a series of walls about fifteen feet high and each thirty to fifty feet long. Behind these walls are the shops and houses, accessible only through gates in the wall. In the wealthier streets there is a high screen behind the gate so that one can see nothing as one passes, except the upper floor, which is often decorated tastefully in lacquer and gold. Most of the streets are lined with shops open to the narrow street. Because of the narrow spaces and the movement, the scene changes continually so that one never really gets a chance to see anything.

"The people stare at us, as we would stare at a Chinese on the street at home. Their expressions show no friendliness but no overt hostility. . . . I think their attitude probably reflects their conservative sense of superiority mingled with an undefined feeling of respect for the foreigner whom they cannot understand. (I would not be surprised if, at this very moment some Chinese were writing in his diary that today he saw some foreigners whose facial expression he would similarly explain.) Most of them pass us by in silence; only the children run around our palanquins with a cheerful 'Chow chow, tubahu' [*sic*] (Hello, big merchant). Only rarely do we hear the hostile cry 'Fayu' (red devil).

"Every corner is interesting. . . . Fishmongers, their wares neatly sliced lengthwise . . . Butcher shops, where hang yellow roasted ducks and dogs . . . Shops where bits of meat and some sort of cakes sizzle in frying pans . . . Basket-weavers . . . Pottery makers . . . Shops offering hand-painted screens and fans . . . Shoemakers . . . and carvers of ivory and jade . . .

"The different tradesmen congregate with each other according to their businesses. . . . There is a Lacquer Street, a Jade Street, a Pottery Street, a Silk Street and so on. Good taste and untiring energy plus native skill make the Chinese into superb handicraftsmen. Their wares are most tempting, especially the embroidered silks and the beautiful ivory carvings, but their prices are even higher than those of the Hindus. They won't come down much, either. Ah Bum, the best guide we have had anywhere, helped me to bargain.

"In the evening, our cross-eyed boat lady took us down the canal to the river to the so-called flower boats. These are houseboats of all sizes, charmingly decorated and fitted out for evening entertainment. Bachelors give their dinner parties here and, through a so-called 'dancing master,' order girls to sing and dance for them. On some of the flower boats, 'dancing girls' sat waiting, each in her little doll's house, pink-robed and heavily made up. They actually look like not very well manufactured toys.

"On the verandas of the flower boats, some people were

94

smoking opium while others enjoyed themselves in various ways I shall not describe. . . .

"The night at the hotel was made unpleasant by the constant shouting of the watchmen. The next morning early we set out in our palanquins to visit the old city. . . . On the gate tower there is a water clock which tells the inhabitants the time of day. . . . We saw the Place of Examinations with its thousands of tiny cell-like structures in which the candidates for government service anually take their examinations. Only forty-seven out of all the thousands pass each year —not by any means the best, but those, we were told, who can pay the most! Then we proceeded to the Place of Execution where the Number Two Executioner showed us his sharp sword and illustrated how beheading is accomplished. . . .

"On the old city wall stand menacing cannon, more dangerous, I suspect, to those who fire them off than to their intended targets. . . . Outside the wall there is a curious collection of quiet little houses; these are the provisional resting places of wealthy Chinese for whom no suitable burying place has yet been found . . . sometimes they remain thus for years. The poorer Chinese keep their sarcophagi in their homes until they can find a burial place for their ancestors.

"Visited a Confucian temple and the Temple of Torture. In the latter, all the tortures of hell are drastically portrayed as a warning to would-be sinners. Nevertheless, there seem to be enough sinners because we saw some prisoners walking around in wooden collars which prevent their ever lying down . . . . Others were in chains. . . . The prison guards, some of them smoking opium, held out their palms for money. . . .

"In the evening, a cozy time with Bose and his wife."

Macao, March 14, 1893: "Left Canton at 8 this morning and arrived here at 4:30 p.m. On the ship there were several stands of guns along the railing for the use of passengers in case of attack by pirates; an armed guard patrolled the deck. Fortunately we did not have to use these weapons; I was more afraid that their ancient barrels might explode than of the pirates.

"Macao is an almost completely dead city, due largely to Portuguese failure to make it into a free port like Hong Kong. In the harbor there are a number of junks and a small steamer that takes passengers to and from Hong Kong. A silk factory, with 300 Chinese women spinning thread from cocoons, seems to be the sole remaining enterprise. And for this remnant of vanished empire: 400 policemen, 150 soldiers, two gunboats, several armored forts, a governor with a salary of $7,000 and various officials! The whole silly business exists only for the few gay uniforms. I figured out that Portugal could save $350,000 a year by giving up this relic in which a few gambling houses and opium dens are the sole beneficiaries."

After a night in Hong Kong spent with German friends, my father boarded the North German Lloyd steamer *Sachsen* for Shanghai. After four days of rough seas in the Formosa Strait, the ship anchored at the mouth of the Yangtze River in a fog so thick that the captain could not see the lighthouse.

"A storm blew up and the yellow waters of the broad river grew so wild that our good ship behaved in a way that reminded me unpleasantly of the trip from Genoa. Finally the fog lifted. The captain proceeded slowly, constantly taking soundings. We passed two steamships at anchor, obviously lost, who, when we passed, pulled up anchor and followed us. The captain showed me the chart on which one could see that the river, miles broad, has only a tiny narrow channel through which ships can pass. At Wusung, a large sandbank prevents big vessels from passing except at very high tide. Here we anchored at 7 p.m. and signaled for the tender which was to take us to Shanghai, but, in spite of signal flares and blasts from the foghorn, no tender appeared until the next morning.

"As we approached Shanghai, there were large factories on both sides of the river; then docks and a long row of big modern buildings. Ships from many countries rode at anchor. Except for the Chinese junks, we might have been landing in a European city. The Bund [main street along the waterfront] with its European buildings looks something like Queen's Road in Hong Kong.

"Good accommodations at the Astor House . . . Took a walk through the main part of the city. . . . The only novelty on the streets was a curious one-wheeled barrow with a seat on each side of the wheel, used for carrying one or two people or one person and his baggage, or for any other kind of balanced load. The coolie who pushes it puts up a small sail to help him when there is a favorable wind! I imagine that this contraption originated in the interior where the roads are too narrow or too bad for two-wheeled vehicles. . . .

"Dinner at the German Club. Afterwards we visited some of the enormous opium dens in which hundreds of addicts lie on their sides smoking until they achieve their escape from reality . . . a horrible sight! The Singsong Houses, half-restaurant and half-brothel, are scarcely more attractive. . . .

"Our guide took us to one place where, at my request, he induced one of the girls to take the bindings off her feet so that we could see what this barbaric habit does to a woman's anatomy . . . her crippled toes and swollen feet almost made me sick. And yet, isn't our tight lacing of a woman's waist just as barbaric?

"Finally we stopped in at a Chinese theater and saw the male actors making up for female roles. We stayed at the performance only just long enough to observe that the actors, all male, frequently turn their backs toward the audience while a

97

coolie wipes their sweating faces with a steaming hot rag. Sometimes they use this interval to spit or blow their noses on the floor before they turn around; the coolie then scuffs his feet over the spot much as a hen scratches gravel!

"The bathhouse where the coolies bathe *en masse* at a price of three cash (about one-third of a cent) per head is an unbelievable sight better left undescribed."

After that evening my father apparently had had enough of the Chinese quarter; he spent the rest of his time in Shanghai being entertained by friends in the European colony. About this he wrote:

"The foreign colony governs and manages itself very well. The Germans, British and Americans operate jointly, the French go it alone and seem to keep to themselves. The Anglo-German-American group has its own police and troop contingents." The diary contains no comment upon the European intrusion into China, which seems taken for granted. Nor is there any reference to the sad state of the Manchu regime. Actually, except for Canton and the native quarters of Hong Kong and Shanghai, my father had seen almost nothing of the vast country which he wrote off as "the gloomy Middle Kingdom," without any apparent realization that a great civilization was dying under the impact of unwanted Western intrusion. His sympathy had been stirred by the people of India. China and its people left him cold, perhaps because he did not see as much of the real China as he had seen of India, or perhaps because he was so impatient to reach Japan.

Japan

March 27, 1893: "At half past six this morning I got up and looked out of the porthole. Through the morning mist looms the outline of a rocky island! Japan, the land of my dreams, lies before me! Quickly into my clothes and up on deck! The activity of the crew shows that we shall land soon . . . no other passengers in sight except for the Chinese up forward. In a few minutes a narrow segment of the sun rises above the rocky island and then the whole fiery red ball. . . . The Land of the Rising Sun! . . . Soon the outlines become clearer . . . small green islands with bizarre shapes . . . an opening appears through the more distant mountains . . . we move quickly towards it . . . a narrow channel opens into a bay surrounded by green hills, some sloping gently, some sharp and sheer. . . . Toward us, across the mirrorlike water, come countless fishing boats with rectangular sails . . . and now a last unexpected turn and we are in the harbor of Nagasaki. . . . The morning mist lifts and the sun shines upon an incomparable picture. After the somber Middle Kingdom it is doubly exciting to see this happily smiling world . . . pennants floating from little ships and from white houses half-concealed in green foliage. And now a web of ropes attaches our ship to two big coal barges while little boats cluster around us. . . .

"I wish I could juxtapose the pictures of two ships coaling —the one in Port Said and the other in Nagasaki. There, everything dirty, sad and brutish; here, everything clean, cheery and graceful. With genial skill the Japanese build a sort of terrace out of bamboo, boards and rope reaching from our ship to the flat barges. This takes about ten minutes. Then a man and a woman take their places on each step and soon little baskets of Japanese coal are flying from hand to hand with incredible speed from barge to ship. When a basket falls and pours its black contents over the workers below, there is happy laughter and badinage that goes on until the next accident.

"Japanese merchants in native costume but with European hats come on board, bow low and present their credentials or offer their dainty wares. They are fabulously polite and just as shrewd. . . .

"After breakfast we climb into a sampan and are rowed ashore, where we are greeted by a crowd of ricksha coolies who politely doff their hats down to the ground and recommend themselves by number . . . we thank them with equal politeness but prefer to walk.

"The German consul gives us a few directions for sightseeing although there is not much to see, and we mount into rickshas. The city is built on a number of islands connected by bridges. One of the islands, Deshima, was for centuries occupied by the Dutch who, alone among the Europeans, were permitted to live and trade there. We were shown the hill where Christians were martyred in the early seventeenth century. We make our way through the clean, small streets and visit several shops where we admire expensive tortoise-shell wares and porcelain. Then up a hill to an old Shinto temple, with the curious torii showing the way. From the hilltop a magnificent view of the charming land and sea . . . before us a quiet garden with great trees and, between them, white cherry blossoms . . . in the midst of this peace, the temple —a row of flat little houses surrounded by trellis . . . a few women are kneeling before the unpretentious shrine . . . a few beggars wait at the gate. . . . We must leave Nagasaki and get back aboard our steamer.

"The lovely passage through the Inland Sea is somewhat spoiled for us by gray, foggy weather. Only when we pass through narrow straits between islands can we really see the shore. They say that the contrasts and constantly changing scenery are absolutely entrancing. From what little we saw, I believe it.

100

"Arrived at Kobe in pouring rain. Mr. Simon [again, probably a Hamburg client] sent his servant to the dock . . . ricksha coolies were waiting with paper lanterns and paper umbrellas, but first all our belongings are taken to the customs inspection. When I asked the inspector (in European uniform) whether I should open anything, he burst into roars of laughter. (That is politeness among the Nipponese: they even laugh when announcing a death; it is rude to show an unpleasant facial expression.) After a brief conversation, the still-laughing inspector lets me through and I go off to the hotel through the pouring rain in a closed ricksha. Mr. Simon very kindly took me to the German Club, where I had a pleasant evening. Tomorrow I must get vaccinated because smallpox is at present epidemic. . . .

"Kobe is essentially a European settlement and therefore not very interesting, although it lies prettily situated on a blue bay surrounded by green mountains. . . . Got vaccinated and paid several calls [presumably on German clients] and visited a waterfall . . . in the evening, a pleasant dinner at Mr. Simon's home.

"Osaka is one of the largest commercial centers of Japan, with 300,000 to 400,000 inhabitants. It derives its importance from the fact that the Shogun Hideyoshi made it his residence. Of the mighty fortress-castle which he erected only the huge foundation walls remain; the rest was destroyed in the revolution of 1868." (This is not accurate. See Chapter One. Osaka was important long before Hideyoshi's time as the stronghold of the commercially active Shin Buddhist sect. Nobunaga besieged Osaka Castle for ten years before he was able to reduce it. Also, when Hideyoshi became the shogun, he made his headquarters in Kyoto.)

"Japan is a remarkable product of contradictions. Centuries-old implements are used side by side with products of modern civilization. Customs resulting from long years of isolation persist under a layer of Europeanism. Osaka, city of little lattice-and-paper houses, has electric light. Two very modern iron bridges span the river that divides the city . . . a few modern business buildings rise against a background of green hills on which stand ancient temples and pagodas. Near the remains of the moated castle are barracks filled with troops in European uniforms. . . .

"After jolting through miles of narrow streets, we came to a charmingly laid-out garden with several small artistically decorated teahouses. Through this miniature park strolled groups of nature-lovers enjoying the tranquil beauty of the scene—black heads, black eyes, colorful kimonos and merry laughter—an entrancing picture. . . .

"At the railway station we had a little trouble buying our tickets to Kyoto because our guide had not arrived from Yokohama."

Kyoto, March 31, 1893: "Arrived here at 8:30 last night. The crowds of Japanese tumbling out of the train, with the women in their wooden getas, sounded like a regiment of cavalry. . . . In rickshas through the cold night air along streets illuminated by paper lanterns . . . in half an hour we reached the foot of the hill on which stands or, rather, up which climbs the Yaami Hotel, a series of ten little houses connected by bridges, with each house at a different level.

"Below my window is a steep drop with dwarf pines and blossoming plum trees. In the distance little white houses climb the green mountains on the other side of the valley. After breakfast we walked up the hill behind the hotel to visit some Shinto shrines. Kyoto seems to enjoy a continuous holiday; we met many Japanese groups walking about and enjoying the tranquillity of a smiling nature, much as we do on Sundays. . . .

102

"After lunch we rode in rickshas to Otsu between fields of rice paddies smelling unpleasantly of night soil . . . then hilly country and a few neat villages until we came to a spot overlooking Lake Bewa. A magnificent view—at our feet the blue lake surrounded by mountains on which there were still some patches of snow . . .

"We climbed down and were shown the place where the Russian Tsarevitch recently had a narrow escape from assassination. Then to a teahouse high up on a little hill. An outpost —a young girl—lay in wait for us at the foot of the hill and invited us to climb up to her mother's establishment. When we accepted, she ran all the way after our rickshas on her clop-clopping getas and arrived panting and laughing in time to welcome us . . . a peasant type with broad head, small nose and oversized chin, but gay and eagerly attentive to our needs. She pours sake, brings a charcoal brazier to warm our hands, offers the tobacco tray and, at each request, hiccups 'Hai!' (yes) and runs off on her bare feet. (We, of course, had removed our shoes as we entered.) She even shows a guest the way to the washroom and waits for him patiently until he has accomplished his mission there. She laughs at everything, in fact, a little too much, and is ready for any kind of joke or teasing."

April 1, 1893: "This morning we shot the rapids of the Hozu River. I don't know which was more impressive—the wild river and the rugged scenery, or the quiet skill with which our three boatmen guided and poled their craft through the dangerous parts of the passage. These sturdy fellows told us that they would have to drag their boat back through the rapids by walking with ropes along the rocky banks or in the stream."

(Seventy-three years later, when our family enjoyed the same adventure, the boat was loaded on a motorized truck to be taken back upstream. It was interesting for us to follow as closely as we could my father's footsteps in the Kyoto-Nara area. A few of the ancient temples and shrines which his diary describes in some detail have been destroyed by earthquakes or fires, but most of them still exist because Kyoto and Nara were mercifully spared from the World War II bombing that destroyed most of Japan's major cities. Since modern guide-books fully and accurately describe these ancient monuments and their history, my father's descriptions are omitted here. I shall quote from the remainder of his diary only a few excerpts which register his reactions to those bits of Japanese life which he encountered and, for the most part, hugely enjoyed.)

During my father's stay in Kyoto, a new section of the Yaami Hotel was opened. (Incidentally, the modern Miyako Hotel, where we stayed in 1966, is built on the same site. Unfortunately the old Yaami guest books no longer exist.) The opening of the new addition in 1893 was the cause of a considerable celebration, attended by guests from as far away as Kobe. There were fireworks and an evening of music and dances.

"The guests," my father wrote, "included the haute monde of Kyoto, dressed for the most part in European costume. It was not surprising that there should be a few errors. One very expensive-looking gentleman came in white gloves, bowler hat and black morning coat, under which he wore a woolen hunting shirt with no collar or tie! He was not the only victim of the urge toward Europeanization. The dancing girls were charming, especially in the graceful movements of their hands. After they had finished their performance, they crowded about the European ladies, giggling and squealing like children. I couldn't help comparing their soft and fluid grace with the Junoesque figure of a tightly-laced American lady. . . ."

An evening at the theater:

"Today being the Jimmu Tenno festival, the streets were so crowded that one could scarcely get through, but a Japanese crowd is always good-natured and gay." (This, unfortunately, is no longer true; in today's Japan, the crowds are just as rude and impatient as they are in Western cities.)

"The theater is an oblong—longer than it is wide. We had a box with a railing. The audience sits on the floor of the pit . . . places marked by little wooden tabs. Shoes are left outside. Around the pit is a gangway at the same height as the stage, used by the actors to represent their going on a journey, or to show off their costumes. The government does not permit men and women to act in the same play, so it has to be one or the other. We were fortunate in seeing a performance in which women took all the parts, and very ably too. . . . An interesting feature was the revolving stage which makes it possible to show two entirely different settings.

"The play itself was most interesting, representing life in the time of the daimio and samurai while at the same time illustrating the peculiar superstition about foxes which still exists among many people in modern Japan. At the end, all the bad people die, especially the women, one of whom kills herself while another is beheaded on stage. During such scenes the ladies in the audience wept as if their own lives were at stake but this did not interfere with their uninhibited gaiety during the intermission. The *souffleur* is on the stage with the book in his hand and alters his position constantly to be near whichever performer he has to prompt. Since almost all the speeches are very long, it is not too difficult to follow the sense of the play. The 'orchestra'—a drum and a sort of hand-violin—sits on stage under a net and provides a melo-dramatic accompaniment. From time to time a voice from the same region makes what appear to be explanatory comments. As this was a festival performance, the evening ended with a superb juggling act."

From Kyoto my father and his friends went by ricksha to Nara, a distance of twenty-seven miles, then mostly through open country. He marveled at the fact that the coolies were able to make this journey in three and a half hours. (Today, Nara and Kyoto are practically one metropolis and it takes about half an hour to cover the twenty-seven miles in an auto-mobile.) What my father liked best about Nara was the peaceful setting of the ancient shrines and the beautiful grove of cryptomeria trees. Again and again the diary notes the ex-quisite taste of the Japanese and their love of beauty. For ex-ample:

"In Kyoto, there is an ancient cherry tree as big as a full-grown beech, propped up by thirty bamboo supports which help the old man to carry his weight. [We searched in vain for this tree.] Each year, when the old man begins to bloom, there is a special festival. Right now the red buds are appear-ing and people are putting up the little bamboo shacks all around for the celebration which young and old will attend in respect for the old man's birthday."

Or again:

"I do not believe that any other people on this earth have so well grasped nature—an open house of God in the midst of a peaceful grove or garden is more beautiful than the most per-fect church or mosque."

In Shizuoka and Nagoya my father visited porcelain, cloi-sonné and lacquer factories as well as silk-weaving and em-broidering establishments. About shopping in Japan, he wrote:

106

"One should go shopping in this country only if one hasn't a cent in one's pocket, if one has no letter of credit and if there is no one from whom one can borrow money—otherwise shopping is likely to be financially disastrous. . . .

"To appreciate the beautiful handicraft products one must see them made and observe how the skillful artisans sit on the floor and patiently create their lovely things. The Japanese is an unequalled observer of nature and has an unparalleled ability to reproduce what he sees in a few powerful lines. What impresses me is that he is free from the European cult of symmetry. He sees in his trees not only the blossoms but the shape of the branches. The slender bamboo, the thousandfold chrysanthemum, the comical stork and every kind of animal give him the inspiration he needs. His creations are a hymn to nature and, because he understands nature, his refined instinct enables him to produce real works of art. The first genial design, seemingly drawn in a few seconds, is then transferred to metal, stone, ivory or silk with incredible patience and care. A little lacquer bowl takes two years to make. One wonders how long that old man with the spectacles will hammer away at his little Damascene steel box, fitting into it each little piece of gold to carry out the design.

"Oh, and the embroidery! I saw pieces of silk more than three meters square so heavily embroidered that one could not even see the background material. They depicted landscapes as beautifully as if they had been painted. The work of years.

"After visiting the workshop, one goes to the salesroom, where friendly and smiling young men spread their treasures on the floor and one is tempted by every piece one sees. Whether or not one buys anything, one can be quite sure that in the evening one will receive a visit, during which new treasures are spread out on the floor of one's hotel room. The visitor asks all kinds of questions—all Japanese have an avid hunger for information—and, after half an hour or so, he makes a deep bow and departs, usually not without having made a sale."

About Japanese women:

"Some older women still follow the ugly custom of lacquering their teeth black and shaving their eyebrows. The young women usually have too little nose and too much chin, but occasionally one sees lovely, delicate faces.

"Married women show great respect for their husbands, to whom they are said to be faithful, but apparently do not expect their husbands to be faithful to them.

"The young girls are impeccably polite, friendly, eager to please and full of fun. They are easy to amuse and, at the same time, ready to depart the instant they feel that they are no longer wanted. For example:

"After dinner at a Japanese inn, the two little maids who had waited upon us sat down at our table to entertain us. Since communications were limited, we played various hand games and tossed little oranges back and forth until one burst, causing delighted laughter. Then we had to empty our pockets and explain their contents. My watch, which shows the day of the week, was a sensation. Finally, after much laughter, the two little creatures bowed to thank us, '*arrigato*,' bowed again to say good night and withdrew like two well-brought-up children.

"And, indeed, the children are well brought up. A four-year-old has the youngest member of the family strapped on its back. If there is no baby, a stone or some other weight is tied on in a sling so that the child will get used to carrying. Even the little ones bow politely when a stranger speaks to them."

Simplicity and cleanliness were two other Japanese characteristics which drew repeated favorable comment from my fa-

108

ther. He described with evident appreciation the austere yet practical and attractive arrangements of a Japanese house or inn:

"The house is not much more than a roof of thatch or Korean tile supported by poles driven into the ground. Its wooden floor is covered by tatami matting pleasant to walk upon in bare or stockinged feet. The four side walls are movable panels of light wood frame, enclosing little squares covered with paper to let in the light. Sometimes the bottom rows of these openings frame pieces of glass to keep out the splash from the frequent rainstorms. . . . Interior partitions are used to divide the house into whatever separate rooms are desired; these, too, are movable.

"A typical room, whether in a private house or an inn, usually contains no furniture beyond a small table and perhaps a few cushions. Mattresses for sleeping are brought out from a low cupboard at night and put away in the morning. At an inn the maid takes care of these simple arrangements and also serves the guest's meals in his room. In cold weather she brings a charcoal brazier. On one wall there is a niche in which there is either a flower arrangement or a single painting, occasionally a little shrine. . . .

"Usually, one door panel slides open to reveal a tiny garden with tastefully arranged small shrubs, rocks, moss and perhaps a miniature pool. . . .

"The maid also takes one to the bathroom and attends to one's ablutions if desired. No people bathe as much as the Japanese, not only for cleanliness but for relaxation and warmth. A large wooden tub is kept constantly full of steaming hot water. One does one's washing before entering it, soaping and rinsing one's body, or having it rinsed with pitchers of cold water. Families will frequently sit in the tub together. The Japanese are not prudish about nakedness. . . . Like most foreigners, I asked for a (more or less) private bath. The first time, the water was so hot that I yelled in pain and the little maid came running with pails of cold water. Thereafter I had sense enough to test the temperature. . . . If one encounters other guests on the way to or from the bathroom or other facilities, one pretends not to see them—just as one pretends not to see the black-gowned scene-shifters in the theater, or the puppeteers who manipulate the almost life-size stuffed figures at a Japanese puppet show. . . ."

The diary records visits to Kamakura, with its Hachiman Shrine and the great bronze Daibutsu (my father was outraged when two English tourists climbed up on Buddha's hands to be photographed)—then visits to the sulphur springs at the seaside town of Atami—to Lake Hakone with the snow-clad cone of the majestic Fuji-san mirrored in its placid waters—and finally to Ejiri, where my father saw the villa of the then still-living last Tokugawa shogun.

"Few people," he wrote to his parents, "have by their resignation brought about such a change as did this old gentleman —not even Bismarck." And with this solitary political comment, the series of letters ends, except for a few fragmentary and not particularly interesting notes about Tokyo.

A photograph which my father sent to his parents tells more about the capital of Japan than anything he wrote. It shows the Ginza—Tokyo's main street—with telegraph poles higher than the little houses and horse-drawn tramcars—a picture which might easily be mistaken for one taken of New York's Broadway in the early nineties. (Today the Ginza is a river of densely packed motorized vehicles flowing—or failing to flow—through a canyon of tall buildings.)

It seems strange that my father, whom I knew as a man of intense political and social interests and of strong convictions, should have been so little troubled by what he saw and heard

110

on his trip to the East. His lack of concern was probably characteristic of the European attitude at the time—an attitude toward the Asian peoples of mingled sympathy and contempt, summarized by Rudyard Kipling in the phrase, "the White Man's Burden." It is true that he was shocked by the English treatment of Indian "natives" and that he found the Portuguese colony at Macao a ridiculous remnant of past glory. But, on the whole, he expressed no disapproval of European imperialism nor any realization of the predatory nature of Europe's intrusion into Asia. The reason is probably quite simple: my father was being trained as a merchant-banker; he visited the family bank's clients wherever he found them on his travels; he was not just a tourist; he was an emissary from the European banking and mercantile world; and it was this very world of commerce and finance that had led Europe into Asia.

Nevertheless, it seems odd that, even as a tourist, he did not sense either the crisis brewing in China or the tide of chauvinistic militarism rising beneath the tranquil surface of Japan.

5

Japan Becomes Aggressive and the United States Enters upon the Asian Scene

In 1894, only a year after Paul Warburg left his "peaceable" Japan, the Japanese attacked China, using the historic route through Korea once followed by Hideyoshi. This time, however, Japan had a navy to protect its communications.

Under the fast-decaying rule of the Manchus, the once-great Chinese Empire was in no position to meet the challenge. The Japanese navy wiped out China's antiquated fleet in the Battle of Yalu, while the army landed in Korea, defeated the Chinese at Pyongyang and captured Weihaiwei in Shantung province.

China sued for peace and, under the Treaty of Shimonoseki (1895), was forced to cede Formosa and the Pescadore Islands to Japan and to recognize Japan's paramount interest in an "independent" Korea. Formosa, after being under Manchu rule since 1683, now became the Japanese province of Tai-

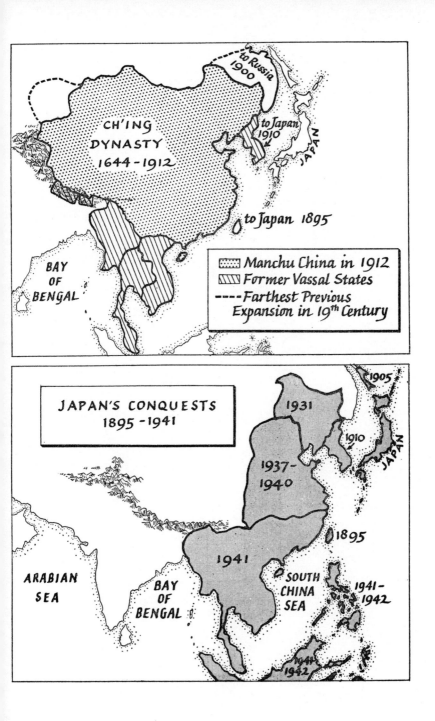

CH'ING
DYNASTY
1644-1912

to Russia
1900

to Japan
1910

JAPAN

to Japan 1895

BAY
OF
BENGAL

▦ Manchu China in 1912
▨ Former Vassal States
---- Farthest Previous
Expansion in 19th Century

JAPAN'S CONQUESTS
1895-1941

1905

1931

1910

JAPAN

1937-
1940

1895

ARABIAN
SEA

BAY
OF
BENGAL

1941

SOUTH
CHINA
SEA

1941-
1942

1941-
1942

wan. (Fifteen years later, Japan formally annexed Korea, making it into the Japanese province of Chosen, without any protest being lodged by Britain or the United States.)

While Japan was thus launching its campaign of expansion, the United States was approaching the climax of its own westward drive across the Pacific—a drive which had begun almost imperceptibly with the westward expansion across the continent, gathering a curious momentum of its own. Ever since the American people had turned their backs upon Europe, it was almost as if they had been propelled westward by a powerful prevailing wind.

The story had begun, much as Europe's eastward drive had begun, with a combination of mercantile search for profit and missionary zeal in which both the adventurers seeking profit and the missionaries seeking to spread Christianity increasingly demanded and received government support.

Early in the nineteenth century, when Yankee traders turned from Atlantic to Pacific adventure, some of them developed a highly lucrative triangular trade based upon carrying Hawaiian sandalwood to China and exchanging it for tea, porcelain and other Chinese products for the American market. The clipper ships were soon followed by whalers, who made Lahaina on the island of Mauwi a convenient repair port. At about the same time (1820) Boston missionaries came to Hawaii to preach Christianity and to promote American influence. (The Hawaiian king, Kamehameha the Great, had just died and his son, Kamehameha II, had abolished paganism and the ancient tabu system, leaving the "heathen" islanders without a religion.) When King Kamehameha III established a constitutional monarchy, President Monroe appointed a "resident agent" to look after the newly established American interests.

During the next decade British and French warships began

115

to visit the islands. In 1842 Secretary of State Webster announced that Hawaii's independence must be respected and that no foreign power should seek undue influence or special privilege. A year later the United States became the first foreign power to establish diplomatic representation at Honolulu.

With the advent of steamships, Honolulu gained further importance as a coaling station and as a potential naval base. California had been annexed in 1848 and admitted as a state in 1850. Soon afterward President Pierce and Secretary of State Marcy began asserting that the "manifest destiny" of the United States was to move westward and influential Americans in Hawaii urged its annexation. Fearing "filibustering" (freebooting) expeditions from California or the promotion of a revolution by Americans in Hawaii, King Kamehameha III consented to annexation on his own terms, which would have preserved a high degree of Hawaiian autonomy, but his death put an end to the project. By this time American sugar interests were firmly established in the islands and, at their insistence, the royal Hawaiian government appealed to Washington for a reciprocal trade treaty. Secretary of State Marcy signed such a treaty in 1855 but the United States Senate, responding to pressure from the sugar growers in Louisiana, refused to ratify it. Again, in 1867, President Andrew Johnson signed a reciprocity treaty and once more the Senate rejected it. In the continuing tug-of-war between the rival American sugar planters, the Hawaiian growers finally won by inducing King Kalakaua to go to Washington, there to make a personal plea to President Grant. The treaty which Grant signed in 1875 was ratified by a Senate no longer dominated by Southern interests and now somewhat fearful that, without a treaty, the Hawaiians might turn to England.

The free entry of Hawaiian products into the United States enormously stimulated the flow of American capital into the

116

islands and the consequent growth of Hawaiian industry; but in 1890 Hawaii lost its favored position when President McKinley's Tariff Act placed *all* sugar on the duty-free list. And now, the American planters in Hawaii openly demanded annexation.

Alarmed by the growing influence of the American planters, Queen Liliuokalani, a stout Hawaiian patriot, attempted to bolster Hawaiian sovereignty by restoring absolute monarchical rule. The infuriated American interests replied by conniving with United States Minister Stevens to engineer the queen's overthrow. With the "moral" support of the American Marines stationed in Hawaii, a "provisional," planter-dominated government deposed the queen and opened negotiations with Washington for annexation. Secretary of State John Foster (maternal grandfather of John Foster Dulles) recommended a treaty of annexation, and President Harrison promptly signed it; but, before the Senate could act upon it, Harrison's term expired and President Cleveland withdrew the treaty, ordering an investigation of the revolution. When Cleveland's agent, Blount, reported that the revolution had been brought about by a conspiracy between the planters and the American Minister, Cleveland ordered the restoration of the queen. The "provisional government" flatly refused to comply with the President's order, converted itself into the Republic of Hawaii, and was soon recognized by the United States as legitimate. (The disgraceful story leaves a number of questions unanswered; among others, why, if President Harrison and his Secretary of State were not involved in the conspiracy, no action was taken by them to investigate the "revolution.")

With the outbreak of the Spanish-American War, the value of an American naval base in Hawaii, plus fear of Japanese designs upon the islands, strengthened the sentiment in

117

Washington for annexation. (By this time roughly one-third of Hawaii's population was Japanese.) On July 7, 1898, Congress passed a joint resolution; President McKinley agreed to it and, on August 12, sovereignty over the Hawaiian Islands was formally transferred to the United States. When Japan protested, it was given the assurance that the rights of Japanese settlers would not be prejudiced.

At this time the United States was already at war with Spain. (Congress had declared war in April 1898 after the battleship *Maine* had been mysteriously blown up at Havana, Cuba.) The Spanish-American War, fought ostensibly for the liberation of Cuba, resulted in the establishment of an American protectorate over the new Cuban Republic and in the outright annexation by the United States of Puerto Rico, Guam and the Philippines.

Up to this point, the United States had remained aloof from European affairs and, by so doing, had been able to expand its continental empire to the shores of the Pacific, as well as to assert its paramount interest over the Western Hemisphere. With the annexation of the Philippines, the United States not only became a colonial power but also entered the European balance-of-power struggle through its Asian back door.

These fateful consequences might have been avoided if the United States had merely liberated the Spanish colonies. Both the Cubans and the Filipinos had for some years been in revolt against Spanish rule. But the warhawks who pushed President McKinley into the war with Spain were not thinking of liberation; they were bemused by "manifest destiny" and dreaming of empire. Among these warhawks were Admiral Mahan, Henry Cabot Lodge and Theodore Roosevelt, the latter destined shortly to become President. Thus, when the Filipinos refused to accept American sovereignty and continued their struggle for independence, an American army was sent to subdue them in a brutal war that lasted three years. The peaceable and pious McKinley rationalized the subjugation of the Filipinos on the grounds that it was America's duty "to civilize and uplift our Little Brown Brothers." (Since the Spaniards had already converted most of the Filipinos to Roman Catholicism, it was presumably not necessary to conquer them to save their souls!)

At this time, when the United States became a factor in the Far Eastern balance of power, Britain was overengaged; she was quarreling with France over Morocco, with Russia over the Near East and fighting a war against the Boers in South Africa. In the Far East, Britain was concerned over Germany's recent entry into the game of carving up China and over Russian designs upon Manchuria. What Britain badly needed was a partner in the Far East to help preserve the precarious balance of power. The United States now appeared as the logical partner, much as it had earlier in the century when Britain needed a partner to keep her European rivals out of the Western Hemisphere. (At that time, quiet talks between Foreign Secretary Canning and United States Secretary of State Rush had led to the pronouncement of the Monroe Doctrine.) But times had changed; the United States was now riding high; McKinley was preoccupied with Cuba and instructed Secretary of State John Sherman to reject a quiet British overture toward cooperation in the Far East. When McKinley was assassinated and John Hay became Secretary of State, he too showed no interest in an alliance with Britain, seeking, instead, to internationalize the open-door policy by general agreement among all the interested powers. In due course, this was to lead to the involvement of the United States in a unilateral guarantee of China's disintegrating territorial

119

integrity—a guarantee both unfulfillable and inconsistent with maintaining the security of the newly acquired American possessions in the Far East.

The Boxer Rebellion

Defeat at the hands of Japan and increasing foreign encroachment, combined with unrest due to drought and famine, set off a revolt against the Manchu government of China. When the Boxer rebels turned their wrath upon the foreigners as well as upon the Peking government, the corrupt and wily Dowager Empress Tz'u Hsi made common cause with the rebels and declared war against the foreign powers. Troops loyal to the regime joined with the rebels in laying siege to the foreign legations. A number of missionaries, the German minister and a Japanese embassy official were murdered. In 1900 eight foreign powers, including the three latecomers—Germany, Japan and the United States—quickly organized an army of 45,000 men, captured the Taku forts and Tientsin and then forced their way into Peking in time to prevent the massacre of foreigners ordered by the empress. Russian troops seized the opportunity to occupy most of Manchuria. The empress fled from the capital in disguise and, in 1901, a heavy indemnity was imposed upon China. Meanwhile, in 1900, Secretary Hay had issued his famous circular which, if it meant anything, meant that the United States would insist upon preserving the territorial integrity of the moribund Chinese Empire.

Japan Attacks Russia

Both Russia and Japan openly coveted possession of Manchuria and Korea. The Russian government had rebuffed a Japanese proposal to divide Korea into Russian and Japanese spheres of influence—prophetically at the thirty-eighth parallel.

Britain shared Japan's desire to contain Russian expansion. Having failed to obtain American cooperation and being impressed not only with Japan's military prowess but also with its progress toward democratic government, London offered Tokyo an alliance in which each country promised to aid the other if, while at war, it should be attacked by a third power. Thus fortified, Japan lost no time. The alliance with Britain was signed in 1902. In 1904 the Japanese navy, without prior warning or declaration of war, fell upon and partly destroyed the Russian squadron at Port Arthur. Japan's army besieged and captured Port Arthur and, a little later, decisively defeated Russia's main Far Eastern forces at the Battle of Mukden. When the Tsar sent his Baltic fleet halfway around the world to retrieve the situation, Admiral Togo brilliantly anticipated its movements and destroyed thirty-two out of the thirty-six Russian warships at the Battle of Tsushima Strait. Although infinitely stronger than Japan, Russia had been forced to fight far away from her center of strength, at the end of the barely completed single-track Trans-Siberian Railway. Prevented by revolutionary unrest at home from bringing his vast European reserves into play in Manchuria, the Tsar decided to accept defeat and to end the conflict.

Japan's victory—the first victory of an Asian country over a European power—had far-reaching effects, but it left the victor exhausted. American sympathy had been with Japan, and American bankers had helped her to finance the war. Now the American government stepped in to help Japan in negotiating a favorable peace settlement. As a fledgling Asian power, the United States was now no longer cooperating with the concession-hungry European nations; it was concerned to assure the safety of its own possessions which might someday be threatened by an unfriendly Japan. It was, therefore, anxious to help Japan to expand on the Asian mainland. The Peace of Portsmouth, New Hampshire, forced the Russians to cede to Japan the southern half of the large island of Sakhalin, and would have permitted Japan to annex the Liaotung Peninsula of Manchuria which had been seized by Russia during the Boxer Rebellion. President Roosevelt sent his Secretary of War, William Howard Taft, to Tokyo to sign a secret agreement (the Taft-Kutsura Agreement of 1905), in which the United States agreed to give Japan a free hand in Korea in exchange for a Japanese guarantee of American possessions in Asia. (At about the same time, Britain and Japan signed another secret agreement exchanging a free hand for Japan in Korea for a free hand for Britain in Tibet.) Three years later, President Roosevelt, still concerned about Japan, had Secretary of State Elihu Root make another secret agreement with Japan, this time exchanging the promise of a free hand in Manchuria for another guarantee of Philippine security (the Root-Takahira Agreement of 1908). In 1910 Japan formally annexed Korea with the tacit consent of both Britain and the United States.

For the time being there was now an uneasy truce among the vultures hovering over the moribund body of the Manchu Empire, parts of which were beginning to break away. Russia was nibbling at Mongolia; Britain was undermining Chinese suzerainty over Tibet. Korea was lost to Japan, which now more than ever had its eyes upon the rich province of Manchuria.

The Overthrow of the Manchus

At about this time liberal-minded Chinese revolutionaries, many of them living outside of China, began to plot the overthrow of the Manchu dynasty and the establishment of a republic. Among them was Dr. Sun Yat-sen, the eventual father of the revolution of 1911. In spite of the weakness of the Manchu regime and the widespread disaffection, it appeared impossible for the Canton revolutionaries to gain control of the country unless they could obtain the support of the powerful Pei-Yang army in the north, commanded by the wily and ambitious Yuan Shih-kai, a general hitherto loyal to the Manchu regime. For this reason, Dr. Sun Yat-sen stepped aside from the provisional presidency to allow Yuan Shih-kai to take over the leadership of the revolution. In the course of four turbulent years, Yuan Shih-kai betrayed the dowager empress, Lung-hu, the Manchu dynasty in the person of the child Emperor Pu Yi, and, finally, the republican revolution. Yuan's idea of a democratic revolution was to make himself into another traditional absolute ruler with a nominally "elected" parliament subservient to his will. During these four years Yuan enjoyed the intermittent support of the monarchical-minded European powers and an international group of bankers greedily seeking railway and other concessions. This antidemocratic foreign intervention rivaled in unsavoriness the early period of the Opium Wars.

At Yuan Shih-kai's death in 1916, China fell apart into warlord domains, with Sun Yat-sen's republican regime controlling only two southwestern provinces of the once-great Chinese Empire. For the next twelve years China was in effect without a government.

123

6

World War I:
A Bungled Peace and
American Irresponsibility

I

THE RISE AND FALL
OF IMPERIAL GERMANY

Japan's rapid rise to power in Asia during the death agonies of the Chinese Empire was paralleled in Europe by the rapid rise of Germany, for the first time united as a nation by Bismarck's wars. With the cautious Bismarck removed from power by Emperor William II, Germany's more aggressive diplomacy was viewed with increasing alarm by its European neighbors. France, isolated after its defeat in the Franco-Prussian War, reached an accord with Russia to offset the menace of a triple alliance between Germany, Austria-Hungary and Italy. At the same time, the French entered into an *entente cordiale* with a British government that had become uneasy over Germany's rapidly growing overseas trade and its naval challenge to British sea power. Actual conflict was narrowly averted in 1911 when President Theodore Roosevelt mediated a dispute over suddenly asserted German claims to part of Morocco. Southeastern Europe was in constant turmoil. The Italians fought the Turks in 1911. Attempts of the Balkan states to establish their independence after Turkey's forced withdrawal led to several conflicts in 1912–1913, and to a clash of interests between Russia and the Austro-Hungarian monarchy. It is well known how that clash led, in August 1914, to a major war which no one, not even the swashbuckling German Kaiser, had wanted. Equally well known is the story of that bloody conflict which destroyed three great empires and altered the map of Europe.

The tsarist empire was the first to fall, when defeat at the hands of the Germans precipitated a long-brewing democratic revolution. In March 1917, Tsar Nicholas II abdicated and was executed in July with his wife and children. A second, more radical, communist revolution in October overthrew the pro-Ally Kerensky government and brought to power Bolshevik leaders who sued for peace, granting vast concessions to the Germans under the Treaty of Brest-Litovsk of March 1918. However, the advantages gained by Germany under this harsh treaty were lost when Germany itself, together with Austria-Hungary, went down to defeat in November of the same year.

The Kaiser abdicated and a new republican German government was forced to sign the Treaty of Versailles. The peace terms imposed upon the Weimar Republic by the victorious Allies were scarcely less harsh than those exacted from Russia by the Germans. President Wilson, who had reluctantly taken the United States into the war barely in time to save the Allies from defeat, labored unsuccessfully for a "peace without victory." The treaties to which he felt com-

125

pelled to agree would, unless revised, inevitably engender future conflict.

The Treaty of Versailles restored Alsace-Lorraine to France and placed the German Saar under international control. In eastern Europe, not only were the German conquests of Russian territory lost but parts of Prussia and Silesia were allotted to a reconstructed Poland. German reparations were set at the impossible figure of thirty-three billion dollars with the idea that the Allies could thus recover the entire cost of the war. (Eventually, only about one-fifth of this amount could be collected.)

The German fleet was sunk at Scapa Flow. Most of what remained of the German merchant marine was seized and divided among the victors. In Africa, German-held Kamerun and Togoland were mandated to Britain and France;* German East Africa was allotted to Britain, and German Southwest Africa was mandated to the (British) Union of South Africa.

By the parallel Treaty of Trianon, the Hapsburgs were expelled from Austria-Hungary and their empire dismembered under the Wilsonian doctrine of self-determination. A part went to form the new Republic of Czechoslovakia. Other parts were attached to Italy, Poland, Rumania and the newly-formed Balkan state of Yugoslavia. Austria itself and Hungary, the linchpins of the old dual monarchy, were reduced to two small, insignificant states.

In the former empire of the Romanovs, all attempts by the British, French, Americans and Japanese to support White Russian factions against the Bolshevik dictatorship failed. A two-year civil war caused great suffering to the Russian people, but the Bolshevik regime survived. Finland, since

---

* As is well known, the mandates were a form of trusteeship set up under the newly created League of Nations.

1809 a part of tsarist Russia, regained its independence as a democratic republic, as did Latvia, Lithuania and Esthonia after two centuries of tsarist rule. Poland, having been wiped off the map by the last of three partitions in 1795, was reconstituted as an independent nation by cession of Russian territory in the east, by German and Austrian cessions in the west and by the grant of a corridor to the Baltic that split eastern Prussia from the rest of Germany.

In the Middle East, the Ottoman Empire, Germany's ally in the late war, disintegrated in defeat under the impact of an Arab revolt stimulated and supported by Britain. The peace treaties imposed upon the defeated Turks confined them to Anatolia; Syria was mandated to France, and Iraq to Britain; a British-protected home for the Jewish people was established in Palestine. Of all the Arab states to which Britain had promised complete independence, only Saudi Arabi achieved this aim. Britain retained direct control of Aden and the Persian Gulf sheikdoms as well as its protectorate over Egypt. In Persia, Britain and Russia were left with competing spheres of influence.

World War I in Asia

Both Japan and China had declared war against Germany, but strife-torn China's contribution had been merely nominal. Japan, on the other hand, had promptly seized the German holdings on China's Shantung peninsula as well as the German-held islands in the Pacific. At the urgent request of Britain, Japan had even sent part of its fleet into European waters.

Concerned over the uncertain internal state of China, and especially over the ultimate disposition of Shantung and the fate of its own leases of Kwantung and the South Manchurian

Railway, Tokyo decided in 1915 to intervene in Chinese affairs. Some of its "Twenty-One Demands" presented to the Chinese government were not unreasonable, but the package as a whole threatened both the European interests and Chinese territorial integrity and independent sovereignty. Since the open-door policy had committed the United States to defend Chinese integrity, Secretary of State Bryan voiced a pious protest. This, however, did not prevent Britain and France from promising Japan in secret treaties that it would obtain the German concessions in Shantung. Nor did it prevent the United States from recognizing (in the secret Lansing-Ishii Agreement of 1917) that "by reason of its geographical propinquity," Japan had special interests on the mainland. (The Taft-Katsura Agreement of 1905 had sold out Korea for the sake of Philippine security; the Root-Takahira Agreement of 1908 had given Japan a free hand in Manchuria for the same reasons; and now it appeared that China would be the next hostage for the American possessions in Asia.)

It was not surprising that Japan should embark with enthusiasm upon the invasion of Siberia when the Allies sought to overthrow the Bolshevik regime in Russia. (This adventure was actually proposed by the United States in its anxiety to preserve the remnants of an anti-Bolshevik Czechoslovak army that had fought its way across most of the Soviet Union.)

At the Versailles Peace Conference, Japan was recognized as one of the great powers and given the mandate over the formerly German-held islands in the North Pacific. However, much to their chagrin, China blocked the Japanese from gaining possession of the former German holdings on the Chinese mainland. Japanese resentment was further inflamed by the rejection of Japan's demand for the inclusion in the League of Nations Covenant of a declaration of racial equality. Britain rejected this proposal largely out of concern for its multiracial empire and particularly out of consideration for Australia's exclusionist policy; President Wilson failed to support it, largely due to the influence of southern members of the American delegation.

Thus, in spite of President Wilson's lofty ideals, the victor's peace imposed by the Allies already contained the seeds of future conflict in Asia as well as in Europe. And, although it would not become evident for some time, European greed and Europe's propensity for internal quarreling had already foredoomed its world supremacy.

II

AMERICAN WITHDRAWAL—
EUROPE'S WEAKNESS

Disillusioned by President Wilson's failure to bring about a just peace, the United States withdrew after 1919 into isolation. The Senate refused to ratify American membership in the League of Nations. The American people endeavored to return to what President Harding called "normalcy," turning their backs upon the outside world.

From 1919 to 1929 the United States enjoyed a period of unprecedented growth and prosperity which greatly benefited banking, the investment business and industry. Farm income, however, declined and labor union membership decreased. The nation's great prosperity was actually only skin-deep; moreover, it was built upon the sands of a delusion resulting from the Versailles Treaty. Britain and France had incurred eleven billion dollars worth of war debts, which they were unable to repay to the United States unless they recovered the cost of the war through German reparations. Although it soon became apparent that it would be impossible to extract anything like thirty-three billion dollars from Germany, the fiction was maintained on both sides of the Atlantic, so that, when President Coolidge was approached concerning a scaling-down of the Anglo-French debts, he replied: "They hired the money, didn't they?" Under President Hoover, American tariffs were raised to an all-time high, making it impossible for the Europeans even to begin repayment of their debts by selling goods to the United States. Practically all of Europe's gold was sucked into the United States. As the United States became more and more prosperous, Europe became weaker and weaker. One by one, the European nations adopted tariffs, import quotas and foreign-exchange controls to protect their economies and their currencies.

Bit by bit, world trade was strangled.

The Rise of Chiang Kai-shek

From 1916 until 1928 the Republic of China existed in name only. The vast nation was split into a multitude of large and small domains, each controlled by a warlord who maintained his private army by unmercifully squeezing the peasants in his area. Some of these warlords were loyal to Peking, some to Canton. In his efforts to establish control over this chaos, Sun Yat-sen toyed with the idea of turning his Kuomintang Nationalist Party into a Soviet-style dictatorship. Under him there rose to a position of high command in the Nationalist forces a young officer who showed political as well as military promise and whom Sun Yat-sen had sent to Moscow on a political mission in 1923. His name was Chiang Kai-shek.

When Sun Yat-sen died in 1925, Chiang, who now commanded the Whampoa Military Academy, became his successor as head of the Kuomintang. (He had married Soong Mei-ling, the younger sister of Madame Sun Yat-sen, about whom it was later said that, while Ching-ling [Madame Sun Yat-sen] loved China, Mei-ling loved power.)

Determined to unify China under Kuomintang control, Chiang moved northward from Canton with his Nationalist army in 1926. Skillfully playing off the warlords against each other and increasing his forces after each successful battle, he succeeded in capturing Peking and in nominally unifying China under Kuomintang control.

Until 1927 Chiang had welcomed the support of the Chinese Communist Party that had earlier been founded under Soviet guidance. Now, however, having disposed of the warlords, Chiang broke with the Communists, launching a murderous purge against them in Shanghai, Nanking and Canton. Nevertheless, by 1931 the Communists, led by Mao Tse-tung, founded a Soviet Republic at Juichin in Southeast China. For three years Chiang launched unsuccessful campaigns against this Communist stronghold. Finally, in October 1933, acting upon the counsel of his German adviser, the notorious General Hans von Seeckt,* Chiang combined an economic blockade with a military attack by an army of four hundred thousand men. After nearly one million people had been either killed or starved to death, the Communists were forced to abandon their base. Roughly ninety thousand of them managed to slip through the Nationalist net and, in October 1934, began the famous Long March, at the end of which they took refuge in the far-northern province of Shensi.

* Von Seeckt had contrived the secret rearming of the Reichswehr during the days of the Weimar Republic.

131

Japan Alienated

During this same period, the United States, under the Harding and Coolidge administrations, took a number of actions that could scarcely have been better calculated to alienate a Japan already disappointed with the treatment it had received at Versailles.

First of all, the United States insisted that Britain abrogate its alliance with Japan. This demand was based upon the strange theory that the United States could limit its naval construction only if there were no alliance between British and Japanese sea power. The American government failed to understand that the acquisition of a Pacific empire had made the United States dependent upon British control of the Atlantic—that ever since the annexation of the Philippines, the United States had entered into what amounted to a tacit alliance with Britain. The Harding administration now proceeded to act upon the strange assumption that Britain was actually a potential enemy. The proper conclusion from that assumption would have been to build a two-ocean navy. The Harding administration, however, wanted to reduce naval armaments and, acting on the premise that it must guard against a possible combined attack by Britain and Japan, it demanded the termination of the Anglo-Japanese alliance and proposed to limit the construction of British, Japanese and American sea power, establishing, as between the United States, Britain and Japan, a ratio of 5-5-3 for capital ships over ten thousand tons. The Washington Naval Treaty of 1922 fixed these ratios (France and Italy each accepting 1.7).

Britain, in the throes of disillusioned pacifism, saw in the limitation of naval construction a much-needed relief for the British taxpayer. Japan accepted because it knew that, without such limitation, the United States could easily outbuild it.

The Japanese knew also that a pacifist United States and a pacifist Britain would abide by the treaty, while the Japanese were free to abide by it only so long as it might suit their purposes. (The United States not only did halt new construction but sank 25 percent of its World War I fleet.) With the Anglo-Japanese alliance severed, the Japanese must have realized that the treaty might someday work in their favor, provided that they might eventually find a partner who would keep Britain occupied in Europe. They understood far more clearly than the American government the nature of the tacit alliance between Britain and the United States. The Japanese accepted the inferior ratio, but they were aware of the hostility toward them which had inspired the treaty.

This was not all. The Harding-Hughes* diplomacy also made an attempt to settle the political affairs of the Far East in such a manner as to prevent any future Japanese expansion. To forestall future Japanese aggression against China, the United States took the lead in internationalizing the open-door policy in a Nine-Power Treaty, signed on February 6, 1922. (Japan's signature did not prevent its invasion of Manchuria a few years later.) Another Harding-Hughes inspiration was an American agreement not to fortify Guam and the Philippines in exchange for Japan's agreement not to fortify the former German islands in the Marshall, Mariana and Caroline groups. (Guam and the Philippines remained defenseless, but the Pacific islands were secretly fortified when Japan later decided upon a war of aggression.) The net result of these actions was to weaken both Britain and the United States and to make Japan fully aware of American suspicion and hostility.

To cap the climax, Congress insisted upon passing the Oriental Exclusion Act of 1924 and President Coolidge signed it,

---

* Charles E. Hughes was at this time Secretary of State.

thus adding a mortal insult to the diplomatic maneuvers which sought to frustrate Japanese ambitions.

The Great Depression

With their government oblivious of the storm signals flying not only abroad but also at home, the American people embarked in the late 1920's upon an orgy of speculative expansion and investment which finally ended in the stock-market crash of 1929, a nationwide epidemic of bank failures and the onset of the Great Depression. A shock wave followed Britain's abandonment of the gold standard in 1931. The postwar house of cards, built upon delusion and irresponsibility, crumbled, spreading economic disaster, unemployment and suffering throughout the Western world.

Asia too was affected. The speculative boom in the price of silver disrupted the economies of India and China. Japan suffered from the strangulation of international trade and from the drying up of the outflow of American capital. Since the war Japan had become the leading industrial power in Asia. Even before the war, in the years between 1877 and 1913, its foreign trade had increased twenty-seven-fold. As the Great Depression hit Japan, discontent engendered pressure for foreign adventure, and a weak China presented an alluring opportunity. In the autumn of 1931 Japan invaded Manchuria. The militarists were now in the saddle.

Japan's seizure of Manchuria posed to the League of Nations the first serious test of the collective-security agreements embodied in the Covenant. The League's failure to meet the test set off the chain reaction that was to lead, eight years later, to the second great world conflict.

7

The Breakdown of Collective Security and World War II

The Rise of Fascism in Europe

Fear that communism might spread to western Europe and the emergence of widespread unemployment under a weakening capitalist system led to the assumption of power in Italy by Benito Mussolini and his fascist Black Shirts in 1922. Most Americans viewed this development with equanimity, praising the Italian strong man for making the trains run on time.

Eleven years later, in a Germany bled white by reparations and runaway inflation, Adolf Hitler came to power, supported by big business and riding a wave of popular resentment against unemployment, the collapse of the banking structure and the *Diktat* of the Versailles Treaty.

In 1935 the League of Nations suffered a second disaster when it failed to halt the Italian dictator's conquest of Abyssinia. A year later a fascist general, Francisco Franco, launched a rebellion against the republican government of Spain, and Hitler occupied the Rhineland in defiance of the Versailles Treaty. France, more afraid of communism than of fascist conquest, had the power but not the will to halt Hitler on his first move of overt aggression. In 1938 the Nazi legions marched into Austria. In the same year Anglo-French "appeasement" of the rising aggressive power of the fascist regimes culminated in the disgraceful betrayal of Czechoslovakia. War had become inevitable.

Under President Hoover, the United States had feebly protested against the Japanese invasion of Manchuria. From 1933 to 1937, President Roosevelt, preoccupied with lifting his own country out of the depression and with instituting his great New Deal reforms, paid scant attention to the rising storms in Europe and Asia. By placing domestic recovery ahead of world affairs, he had wrecked the World Economic Conference held at London in 1933 and destroyed what was probably the Western world's last chance to restore world trade and currency stability.

In 1937 President Roosevelt made an unsuccessful attempt (the famous "Quarantine Speech" at Chicago) to arouse the country from its isolationist lethargy, but many, if not most, Americans felt that if England and France did not consider themselves endangered by the rise of fascist power, there was little reason for Americans to be concerned. This attitude persisted until the fall of France in May 1940.

The Soviet Union was the one country which had remained almost immune to the Great Depression, being more or less isolated from international intercourse by its Marxist experiment in self-sufficiency. The Russians were, however, keenly aware of the dangers posed by the rise of fascism; they alone, during the years of "appeasement," had urged collective action by the League of Nations. In 1938 the Soviet Union had offered to support the Czechs if they should decide to fight for their independence. The Western betrayal at Munich convinced Stalin that the real purpose of Anglo-French diplomacy was to turn Hitler's aggression toward the east.

Japan Invades North China

Meanwhile, Japan, not content with having established the puppet empire of Manchukuo in Manchuria, marched into and conquered northern China, ignoring feeble protests by the League of Nations and the United States. The Axis powers— Germany, Italy and Japan—withdrew from the League. The American government deplored Japanese aggression and the atrocities committed in China by Japanese troops, but continued to permit the sale of scrap iron and oil to the Japanese war machine.

World War II: Europe

It is not necessary to review here the familiar history of World War II that began with the Molotov-Ribbentrop Pact and the invasion of Poland, shortly followed by the Nazi conquest of Denmark, Norway, Holland, Belgium, Luxembourg and France, which left Britain to stand alone against air attacks, threatened by invasion and probable starvation by German submarine warfare. Nor need we recall the painfully slow awakening of the American people, the gradual mobilization of "short-of-war" aid and the great isolationist-interventionist debate which lasted until Japan's attack upon Pearl Harbor. (Had the American authorities been more familiar than they

137

apparently were with Japanese history, they would have been less shocked and surprised by the "sneak attack" which merely repeated Japan's tactics against the Russian fleet at Port Arthur.)

World War II: Asia

Before Pearl Harbor brought the United States into the war, Japan had conquered all of China from Inner Mongolia down to the Yangtze River, as well as Canton and the island of Hainan. Chiang Kai-shek's defeated Nationalist armies— what was left of them—were cooped up in western China with headquarters at Chungking. In addition, the collaborationist Vichy government had handed Japan the keys to French Indochina, thus opening the door into Malaya, Burma and India. One might have thought that these conquests would satisfy even the most rabid of the Japanese expansionists, but the truth was that Japan was hopelessly bogged down in a China which refused to surrender, that its resources were dwindling, that the United States had finally cut off shipments of oil and scrap iron and that the further conquest of southeast Asia had become essential to Japanese survival.

Having, as they thought, taken measures to eliminate American naval power in the Pacific, the Japanese almost simultaneously "sneak-attacked" the Philippines, destroying General MacArthur's air force on the ground, capturing Manila and bottling up the American-Filipino forces on the peninsula of Bataan. Almost without pause, the Japanese attacked Hong Kong, swept into the Straits of Malacca, destroyed a small Dutch-American-Australian naval force, conquered the rich Dutch East Indies and pushed on through New Guinea toward Australia. From Indochina they launched an overland attack through the supposedly impenetrable jungles of Malaya and threatened the last British stronghold at Singapore. Two British capital ships, *Repulse* and *Prince of Wales*, hurriedly dispatched to Singapore's aid, were sunk by Japanese torpedo planes. Thailand (Siam) offered no resistance. Burma fell into Japanese hands. . . . All this happened with incredible speed, and for a few agonizing months it seemed as though Japan had achieved the mastery of Asia.

The fabulous story that began with the Battle of Midway, Guadalcanal, Coral Sea and the Solomons campaign and ended with the island-hopping recapture of Japan's conquests and the destruction of its fleet requires no retelling. Nor is this the place to discuss the final grim chapter of the atom-bombing of Hiroshima and Nagasaki and the Japanese surrender. Like its Axis partners in Europe, Japan suffered a crushing and humiliating defeat, but the fact remains that Japan wrote *finis* to the nineteenth-century chapter of European imperialism.

Japan had not set out to free Asia. Her "co-prosperity-sphere" slogan had merely cloaked her attempt to create an Asian empire of her own. Yet the freeing of Asia and the dawn of a new era were the result of Japan's venture into imperialism. That was not all. From Asia the news of European defeat at the hands of an Asian power would soon sweep into Africa and the Middle East, triggering a world-wide anticolonial revolution.

The Decline of Europe

Two events in 1941—Hitler's sudden attack upon the Soviet Union, and Japan's attack upon Pearl Harbor—marked the turning point of a war which might otherwise have ended with German mastery of the West and a Japanese conquest of

139

the East. As it turned out, the second great world conflict, spawned in Europe like the First World War, ended, perhaps forever, the world supremacy of the western European powers.

In 1945 predominant power was left in the hands of two surviving giants, the Soviet Union and the United States; the one sorely wounded, the other scarcely touched and more powerful than ever. At enormous sacrifice the Soviet Union had provided the major stumbling block to Nazi conquest, while the United States had almost singlehandedly accomplished the defeat of Japan.

Had it not been for Britain's heroic resistance during the year when the island kingdom stood alone, victory over the Axis powers might never have been achieved; but Britain's magnificent contribution to victory could not alter the fact that her days of proud world hegemony had ended.

China Goes Communist

American wartime policy in China had been more or less neutral as between Chiang's Nationalists in the south and Mao's Communists in the North, seeking above all a reconciliation which would produce a stronger effort against Japan. (During most of the war Chiang kept his best troops facing the Communists.) There were two schools of thought: one, led by Major General Claire Chennault, held that Japan could be driven from China by air power and that Chinese troops were not much good; the other, led by Lieutenant General Joseph P. Stilwell, believed that Chinese troops, if properly trained and supplied, would be equal to the Japanese. The Rooseveltian compromise was to "try a little of both." This left each commander feeling that his strategy would have suc-

140

ceeded if supplies had not been diverted by the other. Secretary of War Henry L. Stimson thought that Stilwell was right. However, Chiang Kai-shek could not tolerate Stilwell's crusty insistence upon reforms in the Nationalist high command and eventually demanded his recall. Against Stimson's advice, Roosevelt agreed and appointed Lieutenant-General Albert Wedemeyer as Chiang's adviser.

Thanks to Stilwell and Wedemeyer, a number of Nationalist divisions had been well trained and equipped by the time Japan surrendered. Against American advice, Chiang Kai-shek insisted upon sending these elite troops north to gain control of northern China and Manchuria, where Japanese withdrawal had left Mao Tse-tung's Communist guerrillas in control. This operation was undertaken before Chiang had fully secured his position south of the Great Wall. Nevertheless, in 1945–1946, the Nationalists appeared to be winning. Then, however, the tide turned. Harsh methods of conscription, corruption in the Nationalist command structure and bad leadership led to a series of defeats, with whole regiments and divisions going over to the Communists with their American-supplied equipment.

In a last attempt to bring about a reconciliation and the formation of some sort of a coalition government, President Truman sent General of the Army George C. Marshall to China as a mediator. Marshall's patient efforts failed, partly because the Communists by this time sensed imminent victory, but even more because Chiang Kai-shek stubbornly refused to reform his corrupt and oppressive Kuomintang regime. In late 1946 Marshall returned to become Secretary of State. In the autumn of 1949 Chiang Kai-shek was driven from the mainland and forced to take refuge on Formosa with the remnants of his once-great army. His defeat had been only partly due to bad strategy; even more, it had been due to the fact that he had lost the allegiance of the Chinese people.

The refugee Nationalists were by no means welcomed by the people of Formosa. Indeed, when China had seized the island shortly after the Japanese surrender, there had been a bloody uprising in which some 10,000 Formosans had been killed. Now, the 7,000,000 inhabitants were subjected to the rule of some 3,000,000 refugee Chinese who claimed to be the legitimate rulers of the China they had lost.

8

United States Postwar Policy in Asia

It would be only a slight exaggeration to say that the United States entered upon the postwar period without any policy so far as Asia was concerned, except for a determination to limit Soviet influence as much as possible.

By using the atomic bombs the United States hastened Japanese surrender before the Soviet Union could claim any part of the credit for victory or demand a share in the occupation of Japan.

With respect to China, the United States took a course which actually resulted in driving China into the arms of the Soviet Union. Once the Marshall mission had failed to bring about an end to the Chinese civil war, it would have been the part of wisdom for the United States to withdraw from further involvement. Mao Tse-tung had not yet won Stalin's respect or support. Continued massive aid to the Nationalists until their final defeat served merely to incur the lasting enmity of the Communists without preventing their victory over a regime doomed to defeat by its own incompetence, corruption and unwillingness to reform its antidemocratic character. Unfortunately, by 1947, the Truman administration was committed to a global anti-communist crusade which distorted every aspect of United States policy, especially its policy in Asia.

At the conclusion of the war, the United States occupied a somewhat paradoxical position in Asia. On the one hand, it appeared as the liberator of Asia from Japanese conquest. In an opposite sense, American defeat of Japan shored up the battered prestige of Western man, offsetting the humiliation of the European powers. Both images were dimmed and distorted by the inconsistencies of American postwar policy and action.

The United States appeared as a liberator when it finally freed the Philippines and supported Indian independence. It appeared as a colonial imperialist power when it vacillated over supporting the restoration of Dutch rule in the East Indies and gave outright support to the French effort to re-establish colonial rule over Indochina. The debacle of the Chinese Nationalists, despite lavish American aid, raised doubts as to the firmness of American policy, although the impulse to aid a wartime ally had seemed understandable. What must have seemed incomprehensible to the peoples of Asia was American failure to disengage from the Chinese civil war once its outcome had been settled.

In fairness to the Truman administration it must be said that it probably would have disengaged itself from the lost cause of the Nationalists had not two things occurred. (This was clearly indicated by the White Paper issued by the State

Department in August 1949, by President Truman's statement of January 5, 1950, and by Acheson's on January 12.) One deterrent factor was the outbreak of an irrational anti-communist witch hunt in the United States during which it was alleged that "China had been lost to communism" because the Department of State had been infiltrated by communists or communist sympathizers. "McCarthyism," supported by a well-financed pro-Nationalist China lobby, made it seem politically impossible to cut off the commitment to the exiled Chiang Kai-shek regime as the legitimate government of China.

Even this obstacle to the adoption of a realistic China policy might have been overcome had it not been for the Korean War. Nowhere in Asia was the absence of an American postwar policy more obvious than in Korea. According to the wartime declaration of Roosevelt, Churchill and Chiang Kai-shek at Cairo in 1943, Korea was to be given its independence once Japan had been defeated. But when Japan surrendered, Russian troops had pushed through Manchuria and occupied the northern part of Korea, while American troops liberated its southern half. By prior agreement between the American and Soviet high commands, the thirty-eighth parallel became the line of demarcation between the two occupying forces. Halfhearted American efforts to unify Korea under a non-communist government were frustrated by the Russians, who proceeded to make their zone of occupation into a communist satellite state. The Americans countered by creating the Republic of Korea below the thirty-eighth parallel. Both occupiers agreed to withdraw their military forces at an agreed date. The Russians proceeded to train and equip a North Korean army and then withdrew their own forces. The United States failed to create comparable South Korean forces

145

before it, too, withdrew, the alleged reason being fear that the South Korean president, Syngman Rhee, might attempt to re-unify the country by force.

In June 1950 the North Korean army suddenly invaded South Korea, driving the ill-equipped South Koreans south-ward. At this point the United States intervened with some of its forces stationed in Japan, at the same time appealing to the United Nations to halt the North Korean aggression. Because the Russians were at the time boycotting the Security Council (on account of its refusal to seat China's Communist regime) the United Nations sanctioned the intervention and several of its members sent troop contingents to help halt the aggres-sion. Within a short time the United Nations force under the command of General Douglas MacArthur drove back the in-vaders to the thirty-eighth parallel. So far, so good; the pur-pose of the police action had been accomplished.

Now, however, Truman allowed himself to be persuaded by MacArthur to launch an invasion of North Korea, being assured by MacArthur that, if he did so, the Chinese would not intervene. (This in spite of the fact that clear warnings to the contrary had been given by Peking.) As is well known, MacArthur drove triumphantly northward, announcing that by Christmas all of Korea would be in his hands. But by Christmas 1950 his forces were in headlong retreat, having suffered a humiliating defeat at the hands of the Chinese. Al-though MacArthur had provoked Chinese intervention by driving up to China's most sensitive Manchurian frontier, the Peking regime was branded as the aggressor by the United States and, under American influence, by the United Nations. Thus ended for the time being what hope there had been of developing an American policy based upon the realities of the Far Eastern situation. (As seen by Dean Rusk, then Assistant Secretary of State for Far Eastern Affairs, the "reality" was

that the Peking regime was not the government of China because it was "not Chinese." This was stated in a speech of May
18, 1951.)

At this point it may be useful to note the post-surrender
development in Japan, comparing what has happened in that
country to the post-surrender developments in Germany.

Germany and Japan

Allied planning for the post-surrender treatment of Germany was rendered extremely difficult by the absence of a con-
sensus as to how the problem should be handled. Not only
were there wide differences of opinion among the United
States, Britain, France and the Soviet Union, but within the
United States no clear concept had been developed. The wartime "agreements" reached by Roosevelt, Churchill and Stalin
at the conferences of Teheran (1943) and Yalta (1945)
were incomplete and in many important respects ambiguous.
As a cleavage developed between the Soviet Union and the
Western powers because of Stalin's expansionist policy in
eastern Europe, Germany became a bone of contention between Russia and the West. This doomed to failure a plan of
cooperative four-power occupation hastily and not too wisely
adopted at the Potsdam Conference of July-August 1945.*

No such obstacles stood in the way of the post-surrender
treatment of Japan. Unlike the ill-fated four-power occupation
of Germany, the occupation of a defeated Japan proceeded
smoothly, relatively little affected by the Cold War that split
the victorious coalition in Europe. In fact, because of this Eu-

---

* See my *Germany—Bridge or Battleground* (Harcourt Brace, New
York, 1947), and its sequel, *Germany—Key to Peace* (Harvard Univ. Press,
Cambridge, Mass., 1953).

ropean Cold War the United States used its predominant power in the Far East to deny its allies all but a nominal voice in the post-surrender treatment of Japan. The basic terms of peace had been settled during the war by Roosevelt, Churchill, Stalin and Chiang Kai-shek; they involved the return to China of all Chinese territory, including Manchuria, as well as Formosa and the Pescadore Islands, while Russia was to receive back from Japan the Kurile Islands and the southern half of Sakhalin as well as certain rights with respect to the Port of Dairen and the Manchurian railway system. Korea was to be given independence. Hong Kong was to be returned to Britain. The mandates over the Marshall, Mariana and Caroline islands in the North Pacific were to be turned over to the United States. These terms were eventually carried out by the peace treaty, negotiated without Chinese, Indian or Burmese participation by the United States and other interested nations in 1951. The Soviet Union did not sign the treaty. By that time the situation in Asia had changed in many important respects.

India, Burma and Ceylon had been granted independence by Britain; India had been partitioned and war had broken out between Hindu-dominated India and newly created Moslem-dominated Pakistan over possession of Kashmir. The Dutch had reluctantly agreed to withdraw from the East Indies and to grant independence to a new nation to be known as Indonesia. The French with American help were attempting to reassert their colonial rule over the Indochinese states of Laos, Cambodia and Vietnam.* In China, Mao Tse-tung's Chinese

---

* France annexed Vietnam (Annam, Tonkin and Cochin China) and the neighboring kingdoms of Laos and Cambodia during the 1880's. Prior to that time the Indochinese states had at times been independent, often at war with each other and, for the better part of their known history, either fighting Chinese domination or subjugated to it. For over one thousand years Vietnam was actually part of the Chinese Empire under the Han and T'ang

People's Republic was firmly established at Peking and in full control of the mainland. The United States was still un-

---

dynasties (*ca.* 110 B.C. to *ca.* 900 A.D.). In the thirteenth century the Vietnamese successfully resisted Mongol conquest, and Cambodia became an important kingdom. Later, under the Ming and Manchu dynasties, the Indochinese kingdoms were tributary vassal states, occupying a status similar to that of Korea. (See Chap. 6 of Fairbank, Reischauer and Craig's monumental work, *The Modern Transformation of East Asia*, Houghton Mifflin, Boston, 1965.)

In 1941 the collaborationist Vichy government of France offered no resistance to Japanese conquest, but the Vietnamese did resist and were aided by the United States Office of Strategic Services, which established friendly relations with the Vietnamese leader, Ho Chi Minh. After the defeat of Japan, British and Kuomintang Chinese forces temporarily occupied Indochina, pending the return of the French. (President Roosevelt unsuccessfully advocated placing the former French colonies under United Nations trusteeship until they were ready to become independent nations, but yielded to the pressure of his French allies.) When China "went Communist" in 1949, the Truman administration became alarmed over possible Chinese encroachment upon southeast Asia and extended massive aid to France in its effort to subdue a nationalist rebellion against the reimposition of colonial rule. (Ho Chi Minh, while a convinced communist, was far more friendly toward Moscow than toward Peking, but Russia was far away and the necessities of war actually drove Ho into the arms of China.) The United States bore about 80 percent of the cost of the eight-year-long unsuccessful French effort to re-establish colonial rule, and came close to actual intervention with its own armed forces. It was only because President Eisenhower overruled Secretary of State Dulles, Vice President Nixon and Chief of Staff Admiral Radford that American forces were prevented from entering the combat when the French faced certain defeat. After the surrender of Dien Bien Phu and French withdrawal from Indochina, the Geneva Accords of 1954 supposedly established the independence and neutrality of the Indochinese states. The United States did not sign the Geneva agreements, but promised to respect them. For what happened since that date see the following:

Bernard Fall, *Vietnam Witness* (Praeger, New York, 1966)

Jean Lacouture, *Vietnam Between Two Truces* (Random House, New York, 1966)

Marcus Raskin and Bernard Fall, *The Vietnam Reader* (Vintage Books, New York, 1965)

The Vietnam Hearings, Senate Foreign Relations Committee (Vintage Books, New York, 1966)

Memorandum of Law, Lawyers' Committee on American Policy Toward Vietnam (38 Park Row, New York, 1965)

Arthur Schlesinger, Jr., *The Bitter Heritage* (Houghton Mifflin, Boston, 1967)

For my own views, see Chap. 10 of my *The United States in the Postwar World* (Atheneum, New York, 1966).

willing to recognize its legitimacy, blocking its admission to the United Nations and insisting that Chiang's Nationalist Republic of China on Formosa constituted China's legitimate government and that it was entitled to occupy China's seat in the world organization. In Korea the war had reached a stalemate at approximately the thirty-eighth parallel.

These, briefly stated, were the circumstances in which John Foster Dulles, soon to become Secretary of State under President Eisenhower, negotiated a peace treaty for Japan.

While American philosophy concerning the treatment of the defeated Axis powers was reasonably consistent, the circumstances surrounding the European and Asian settlements were so different that there appeared to be little similarity between the postwar treatment of Germany and the postwar treatment of Japan. Yet this was actually not the case. The aim of the United States with respect to both Germany and Japan was essentially magnanimous—not to punish the peoples of the aggressive nations but to rid them of a leadership which had led them into aggression and to create those social, political and economic conditions which would in future prevent any such leadership from ever again coming to power. In both Germany and Japan, this aim required the stimulation if not the actual imposition of a social, political and economic revolution.

In Germany this objective was difficult to achieve because Germany almost immediately became a battlefield in the Cold War between the Soviet Union and the West, and because not even the three Western occupation powers could agree among each other as to what sort of a "peace-loving," democratic German nation they desired to create. All four of the occupying powers agreed that the major war criminals should be brought to trial and punished, and that those who had actively supported the Nazi regime should be barred from participation in the future political life of the country. But that was about as far as four-power agreement carried. The four powers disagreed over reparations and over what were to be a truncated Germany's physical frontiers. They disagreed as to whether Germany should have a federal constitution like that of the United States, or whether it was to be governed by strong centralized authority. Their disagreements eventually led to the partition of Germany into a Western-dominated Federal Republic and a Soviet-dominated East German "Democratic Republic." Worst of all, the heating up of the Cold War and the partition of Germany led each side to rearm "its Germans," although both sides had originally agreed that one of the essential conditions for future peace was to keep Germany demilitarized.

No such difficulties existed with respect to Japan because, profiting from its experience in Europe and from the fact that neither the Soviet Union nor its other allies had made any significant contribution to the defeat of Japan, the United States assumed what amounted to sole control of the occupation. It was, therefore, in a position to punish, purge, reform and rebuild according to the carefully worked-out plans prepared in Washington prior to surrender. The spectacular success of the American occupation was not due solely to the wisdom of these plans or even to the fact that, in General MacArthur, the United States was fortunate to possess a proconsul ideally suited to the demands of the situation. The success was due in large measure to the way in which the Japanese cooperated with the American authorities.

Unlike Germany, which had never had a wholly indigenous voluntary democratic revolution, Japan had of its own free will cast off its feudal structure during the Meiji period, adopting many of the Western principles of democratic government. It was true that the militarists had arrested and dis-

151

torted this earlier trend toward democracy and that the Japanese people had allowed themselves to be led into expansionist adventure by a series of powerful military fanatics. But the spirit of liberalism, although brutally suppressed during the war, had remained latent; it was ready to be rekindled once militarism was discredited by calamitous defeat.

There was another important difference. The destruction and suffering endured by the German people through Hitler's war left a defeated Germany badly battered but still in possession of remarkable powers of recuperation. There was enough industrial machinery left in Germany for the occupiers to quarrel over; there was enough coal, provided only that the occupiers would allow it to be mined. Defeat left Japan with its cities destroyed, with its people starving and without any of the material essentials for reconstruction. The Germans could feel—and many of them did—that they might well have won the war—that Hitler's great sin had been not to start the war but to lose it. Defeat left the Japanese people convinced that they had been irresponsibly led into a war impossible to win. Finally, for the Germans, defeat was not a new experience. The Japanese were humbled for the first time in their history. Japanese humiliation was real—far more so than that of the defeated Germans; and they were far readier than the Germans to take a hand in reforming their entire social, political and economic structure.

After some debate the United States had wisely decided not to force the Emperor of Japan to abdicate but to retain him as a traditional symbol of loyalty and respect, while vesting the powers of government in a Diet elected by universal suffrage. (Eventually the emperor of his own free will denied his divine origin.)

The new constitution drafted by the Japanese with American assistance provided for an independent judiciary and a ministerial government responsible, like that of Britain, to the popularly elected Diet. Whereas the new West German constitution, adopted at about the same time, provided that the chancellor (prime minister) could be forced to resign only if the Bundestag (House of Commons) agreed beforehand on a successor, the Japanese constitution gave the prime minister and his cabinet no such protection, allowing the Diet to force the government's resignation at any time by a vote of no confidence. In this respect the Japanese constitution provided a stronger safeguard against a reversion to authoritarianism than did that of West Germany.

In both Germany and Japan economic power had become concentrated in a small number of giant combines. In both countries, in spite of wartime controls, these monopolistic agglomerations had prospered. And in both countries the United States endeavored to break up the monopolies and to bring about greater economic as well as political democracy. This effort was far more successful in Japan than in West Germany. In one way or another, the West Germans succeeded in circumventing much of the imposed economic reform and in re-establishing many of the old concentrations of capital and industrial control. (The Krupp empire serves as the most flagrant example.) In Japan, on the other hand, the Zaibatsu empires of the Mitsuis, Mitsubishis and Sumitomos were effectively broken up; there were new concentrations but these centered about a number of banks and were not controlled by the old monopolistic family hierarchies.

Both Germany and Japan went through a period of postwar hardship. Both received generous American aid, largely inspired by the Cold War in Europe and by the Korean War in Asia. Both countries achieved an "economic miracle" of recovery—the Germans more quickly than the Japanese because they started from a more favorable position.

153

Twenty years after their defeat, the two nations most responsible for a catastrophic world conflict had become the leading industrial powers in their respective parts of the world. Both owed this strange reward for aggression to the Cold War. But the division of the world into communist and anti-communist orbits left both Germany and Japan with serious political problems.

Partition left some seventeen million Germans under communist rule. Neither they nor the fifty million more fortunate West Germans were represented in the United Nations. (Japan was admitted to United Nations membership in 1956.) The existence of Western enclaves in Berlin, in the heart of their comunist satellite state, was considered by the Russians "a bone in the throat," while the mere existence of the East German communist state remained an intolerable situation in the eyes of the West Germans. In spite of its prosperity and its favored position as the keystone in the arch of western European defense, the Federal Republic of Germany uncomfortably felt itself to be the ward of the United States, especially after the dream of a united western Europe had been shattered by the resurgence, under President Charles de Gaulle, of an anachronistic French nationalism. Frustrated in their hope of becoming "good Europeans," the West Germans showed unpleasant symptoms of a dangerous reversion to their own form of nationalism.

The political problems posed to Japan by the Cold War were somewhat less serious but they too contained the seeds of future trouble. Under its new constitution, Japan had renounced war and undertaken not to reconstitute its armed forces except for a limited defense organization. A United States-Japan security pact, signed together with the peace treaty, guaranteed Japan against aggression, giving the United States the right to maintain defense forces in Japan proper and to make Okinawa in the Ryukyu Islands into a major American base with "residual sovereignty" over the islands remaining with Japan. Thus, although the security pact was revised, a demilitarized Japan became even more dependent for its security upon the United States than a remilitarized West Germany. Inevitably, this situation aroused mixed feelings among the Japanese: on the one hand, they were happy not to be burdened with the cost of maintaining their own defense establishment; on the other hand, they increasingly resented the political restrictions that their dependence upon the United States imposed upon their foreign policy.

As we prepared for our trip to the Far East in the early summer of 1966, it seemed to me that an interesting antithesis was developing in the international postures of West Germany and Japan.

The Bonn Republic, with powerful armed forces of its own, was desperately clutching at the continued presence of American troops on its soil. Japan, with almost no armed forces of its own, was becoming increasingly resentful of the American military presence on the home islands and in the Ryukyus.

Bonn, with its unrealistic and unimaginative foreign policy at a dead end, was clinging to the clichés of the Cold War and the nightmare of a Soviet invasion.* Japan was moving cautiously toward economic cooperation with the Soviet Union and was increasingly anxious to heal the breach between itself and its powerful Chinese neighbor from whom so much of its cultural heritage derived.

Germany, prosperous and self-centered, was a reluctant and niggardly participant in aid to the underdeveloped countries of the world. Japan, with its far smaller resources,

---

* Since this was written, a new coalition government in Bonn has given some evidence of a new orientation toward eastern Europe, and of less dependence upon American protection.

seemed to be moving toward active leadership in the effort to narrow the gap between the rich and poor nations, as witness its contribution of two million dollars to the Asian Development Bank.

A partitioned Germany remained, though not entirely through its own fault, a major obstacle to peaceful settlement. Japan, slowly feeling its way toward an independent foreign policy, seemed likely to become an active force for international reconciliation and the establishment of enduring peace. About this we hoped to learn more during our impending voyage of exploration.

9

Pilgrimage to the Orient in 1966

A sea voyage is always an excellent preparation for visiting unfamiliar lands. One has time to read history and guide-books and perhaps to pick up snatches of unfamiliar language. This was doubly true of our voyage across the Pacific in the summer of 1966, because the passengers on the *President Wilson* constituted a ship's company almost like the personnel one might choose for a seminar on Far Eastern affairs.

An American missionary family, long resident in Japan, was returning from a visit to the United States. Several American university professors—historians and language specialists—were taking their families to the Far East for the summer, as was one of the foremost authorities on the economy of modern Japan. A Japanese scholar who had been teaching at an American university gave those of us who were interested daily lessons in the difficult language of Japan. Two middle-rank officers of the American State Department's Foreign Service were traveling with their wives and children to new assignments—one in Hong Kong, the other in Thailand. One of them had served a stretch in Saigon. Most of the remainder of the ship's company consisted of United States Navy, Air Force and Army personnel of fairly high rank on their way to Japan, the Philippines or Vietnam. Some were old Asia hands; others were going out for the first time. There were American children of all ages and a few Chinese, Japanese and Filipinos.

Inevitably, the war in Vietnam constituted a major topic of conversation. Two American women—one an English teacher and the other a Y.M.C.A. organizer—set up a discussion group at which I was invited to debate United States policy in Asia with one of the State Department officials. A surprisingly large audience—about a hundred people— participated in a lively discussion between "hawks" and "doves" in which everyone kept his temper, except one superpatriotic businessman, an ex-naval officer, who wanted the United States to bomb China.

In many years of ocean travel I had never encountered a more informed or more informative ship's company. We gained quite a little knowledge of Japanese customs from our missionary friends and from the Japanese professor. From the Princeton economist* I gleaned extremely useful information concerning Japan's industrial and economic development. Our military friends gave us an interesting picture of life in the American bases in Asia—those curious, semi-isolated and self-sufficient American enclaves which now dot the Far East.

---

* Professor William W. Lockwood, author of *The Economic Development of Japan* (Princeton Univ. Press, Princeton, N.J., 1954) and a number of recent pamphlets, one of which he very kindly gave me.

What with these contacts, with rereading Ambassador Reischauer's admirable books on Japan and with doing my homework for the daily briefing of the family on the outlines of Asian history, the time at sea was well spent.

On the way out to Hong Kong, our ship stopped for a day at Honolulu, where we planned our later visit to the islands, and for another day at Yokohama, which gave us our first glimpse of Japan. The latter was used to visit the Hachiman Shrine and the great bronze Daibatsu at Kamakura, to see the beach where Kublai Khan's envoys were beheaded and to have lunch at a Japanese inn. (After we had sat or knelt uncomfortably on tatami mats, watching the interesting preparation of our lunch and then trying, not very successfully, to eat it with unfamiliar chopsticks, we saw on our way out of the inn a party of Japanese businessmen sitting comfortably on chairs and eating "European style" in an adjoining room!)

Yokohama itself we found unimpressive except for its vast extent. I could not help wishing that, like my father, we had first touched Japan at Nagasaki.

Four more days at sea brought us to Hong Kong, where we stayed while the *President Wilson* went to Manila and back, returning to her for the voyage back to Yokohama. Then for three weeks we roamed Japan, following for the most part in my father's footsteps, except that we added a visit to Hiroshima. Japan Air Line took us back to Hawaii, where for ten days we explored the four major islands. Then home by air— in all, a trip of just under two months.

Hong Kong

Arriving by sea, we had the same thrill over the landfall and the beautiful entrance to the harbor that my father had enjoyed years ago. (One misses much if one travels only by air.)

Since 1893 the British Crown Colony had grown enormously in area and population. Kowloon, on the mainland, undeveloped in my father's day, had become a city at least as large as Victoria; and the New Territories, acquired under a ninety-nine-year lease in 1898, had added miles of farmland and waterfront to the colony, so that the mainland almost overshadowed the original city on the island of Hong Kong. Nevertheless, Victoria, too, had grown mightily. Along the waterfront, where my father had admiringly noted "a four-story hotel," there were modern skyscrapers, hotels and apartment houses. The old town hall was dwarfed by huge banks, one of them the Bank of the Chinese People's Republic. The Peak was more thickly settled, with the old funicular tram still operating and the steep streets of the Chinese quarter apparently unchanged. There were no palanquins and the few rickshas, existing for the benefit of tourists, stood waiting in patient rows, like the horse-drawn hansom cabs at New York's Plaza.

The harbor, with its ships from all lands, its ferries and its picturesque junks and sampans, was much as my father described it, except that Diesel and gasoline motors had supplanted steam engines and almost driven sails out of use—almost, but not quite; there were still here and there high-sterned junks proceeding under latticed sail.

The great change was on the mainland where Kowloon had come to rival Victoria as a shopping and commercial center and where something like half of Hong Kong's four million inhabitants now lived, many of them refugees from China. (Only about 5 percent of Hong Kong's population is non-Chinese.) By no means all the refugees are escapees from Communist China; many fled the old China because of famine or unsettled conditions; most of them came from the provinces of Kwangtung and Fukien.

In Kowloon my family had its first view of a frightening phenomenon which plagues the modern world, the growth of shantytowns in and near the big cities—miserable clusters of tin-roofed huts inhabited by poor peasants who have left the land to seek employment in the cities. (One sees these *barrios* all over Latin America and in some parts of Europe and the Middle East.) In Hong Kong and especially in Kowloon these wretched dwellings cluster on the more inaccessible slopes of hills, often in the midst of regions otherwise inhabited by villas and apartment buildings. The colonial government has done its best to provide employment and to build low-cost housing. Many of the refugees now at least have access to water and sewerage, but even the new housing has a sad look, with laundry hanging outside of every window of the four-story oblong concrete boxes, each containing many one- or two-room apartments into which whole families are crowded.

In the New Territories we saw something which my father had not seen during his visit to China. Here were farms worked by peasants in exactly the same manner as farms have been worked for centuries in the arable parts of China. And here were villages hundreds of years old and little groups of fishermen's houses along the shore, and boat colonies where hundreds of thousands of people live on junks and sampans. These boat people are born and die on their little floating homes, going ashore only to sell their fish and to buy the few things they need. They belong to two ancient tribes, the Tonga and the Hoklo, who have lived in this manner along China's coast since time immemorial. (I was told that the Communist regime is now trying to induce them to live ashore.)

The land people are part Cantonese and part Hakka. Being the original settlers, the Cantonese leased the best farmlands

161

from the government. The Hakka (the name means "guest people" or "strangers") came somewhat later and for a time fought with the Cantonese. Now they farm peaceably, side by side, plowing with their wooden plows drawn by water buffaloes, seeding their rice paddies by hand, harvesting and threshing by hand, and carrying water or night-soil in pails suspended from bamboo yokes. Of late, vegetable patches have begun to appear among the paddies, mostly taro and beans. Almost all the farm work is done by women—little dark-clad figures under large round straw hats with a four-inch fringe of black cotton. They dislike being photographed. There are almost no men to be seen; most of them go away to find jobs and occasionally send home money. A centuries-old walled village appeared to be occupied solely by old women and children. The children throughout the New Territories are wretchedly clad and beg distressingly for pennies. One little girl with a baby sister on her back held out the infant's hand for coins.

Men are in evidence among the boat people and in the fishing villages but here too the women seem to do most of the work. The stench in the narrow lanes is overpowering—a mixture of night-soil and fish.

As we stood within a few yards of the narrow river that separates the New Territories from the Chinese People's Republic, I wondered to what extent peasant life there had changed and whether these people would or would not be happier if they happened to live on the other side of the border.

Kowloon is a shopper's paradise. It is also the Western world's chief China-watching station. While my family explored the alluring wares to be found in the arcades, I interviewed a number of journalists—some European and some Asian—who had recently visited the realm of Mao Tse-tung.

All these observers agreed that, in a material way, the vast majority of the Chinese people were better off than they had ever been before, especially the women. An Austrian news photographer said that he thought that, for the first time in their long history, the Chinese people felt themselves to be part of a single nation. He was particularly impressed with the spirit of enthusiastic cooperation which seemed to have supplanted individualism and parochial regionalism. On the other hand, several observers felt that, with the spread of literacy, there was a growing resentment of regimentation and thought control, particularly among the intellectuals. There was general agreement that the regime feared what my Austrian friend called "embourgeoisement" and what others referred to as "revisionism." It was felt that some sort of a quiet purge was going on within the ranks of the party. (This was in July 1966; a month later, the "cultural revolution" was no longer going on quietly and the Hong Kong China-watchers were sending out daily reports of a struggle which threatened to erupt in a civil war.)

Asked whether they considered the Mao regime expansionist or aggressive toward China's neighbors, all but one said about the same thing: "The Mao regime would be aggressive, especially with regard to Taiwan, if it had the military power to challenge the United States. At present China lacks not only nuclear capability but also transport. Trucks are scarce and manpower is still the prime mover." The lone dissident expressed the view that the regime had so much "on its plate" at home that only fear of attack would make it externally aggressive; he added that, with further progress at home, the regime might mellow, as had the Soviet regime. My friends were unable to say whether China actually feared an attack by the United States, but they unanimously declared the belief that, if the United States were to invade North Vietnam, this would almost certainly be considered a prelude to an attack upon China.

Some of the China-watchers were familiar with the positions I had publicly taken in opposition to American policy with respect to Asia and tried to switch our talk to Vietnam. I told them that I prefered to get them to talk about China. All of us agreed that no useful purpose could be served by continuing to treat China as a pariah; that Peking would probably never assume a less hostile attitude toward the United States so long as the Taiwan issue remained unsettled; and that the war in Vietnam should be de-escalated rather than raised to more dangerous dimensions. A Hong Kong Chinese journalist expressed the view that Lin Piao's recent rhetoric about world revolution had been taken much too literally— that "the Chinese Dragon's breathing fire covers his absence of teeth."

A woman journalist from Australia emphasized, as the three things that had most impressed her, the rise of literacy, the emancipation of women and the widespread program of planting trees. "Most of China used to be yellow," she said. "Now it is turning green."

From a few conversations at the American Consulate (and from earlier shipboard talks with Foreign Service officials), I became convinced that it is not true, as is frequently alleged, that the United States government "knows nothing about what is going on in China." Officials naturally feel duty-bound to defend their government's policies and, indeed, do so with all the well-known State Department clichés, but one gains the impression that many of the well-informed Foreign Service officers have their doubts about the wisdom of our policy toward China and about our involvement in Vietnam. Washington knows perfectly well that, until the outbreak of the "cultural revolution," China had made great progress since the disastrous "Great Leap Forward" of the late 1950's. It knows that Peking's foreign policy has been far more cautious than its rhetoric. One cannot help wondering whether the top policy-makers in Washington are not more inclined to believe in their hopes and in their own propaganda than in the information they receive from their outposts.

We had planned a one-day excursion by hydrofoil to Macao, that moribund little remnant of Portuguese empire in Asia, but this plan had to be abandoned when a small typhoon swept suddenly into the area. It was interesting to see how, as soon as the warning was broadcast over the radio, sampans, junks and all manner of small craft scurried into one of the well-protected typhoon shelters maintained by the government.

As we boarded our ship the next day, I think we all felt that we had learned quite a little. We had seen perhaps the best example of what remains of British Colonial rule—a Chinese city of millions governed by a handful of Europeans. We had observed the tremendous gap between living conditions in the small Anglo-Western colony with its schools, fine houses (some of them owned by wealthy Chinese), its clubs, numerous servants, luxury hotels and huge office buildings, and the squalid life led by the millions of Chinese under a benevolent, efficient but overburdened foreign government. This contrast was perhaps most marked in the juxtaposition of the elegant suburb of Repulse Bay with the adjoining, poverty-stricken and filthily reeking boat colony at Aberdeen.

More important, we had had a glimpse of that vanished Old China which my father had found so depressing; and we had vicariously gathered a few impressions of the New China that was now a forbidden land to Americans.

All of us felt a sympathetic liking for the few Chinese with whom we came into contact, perhaps largely because our driver-guide, a well-educated and humorful Chinese, named Johnson Foo, had a real love for his native city and its people. While the country people were aloof, the urban Chinese were uniformly friendly and courteous without being in the least subservient.

One thing that we noticed with surprise was the almost complete absence of flowers. There was magnificent beauty in the rugged, mountainous landscape, in the busy harbor and in some of the delicate products of patient Chinese artists and artisans. But there was also much ugliness both in the city and in the surrounding countryside. Worst of all were the shanty-towns, the poverty of the boat people and the countless neon signs that made the night hideous.

As a student of history I could not help wondering how China would have developed during the nineteenth and twentieth centuries if the Western nations, motivated as they largely were by selfish greed, had not helped decadent and corrupt Manchu rulers to suppress rebellions and thus delayed China's political development. Granted that Confucian China was probably bound to fall of its own static immobility and the decay of the moral concepts which had held it together for thousands of years, what would have happened had the Tai P'ing Rebellion succeeded? Or if Sun Yat-sen, rather than Yuan Shih-kai, had received Western assistance?

As for the future of the British colony, one wonders how long it will suit Peking to permit it to exist on Chinese soil. The lease on the New Territories expires in 1997, but no one in the colony seems to be giving this much thought; new buildings are being erected and land development proceeds as if there were no doubt as to the future. Undoubtedly it suits Peking for the time being to have Hong Kong exist as an entrepôt for a large part of China's foreign trade. (No such reason exists for Chinese acquiescence in the continued Portuguese possession of Macao.) Nevertheless it gives one a curious feeling to realize that at least half of Hong Kong's water supply is piped down from the mountains of Communist China and that the colony exists on sufferance.

Japan

The Japan we saw in 1966—like the Japan Paul Warburg saw in 1893—was a nation only twenty-odd years removed from a major turning point in its history. My father saw an apparently peaceable Japan in the first enthusiastic state of Europeanization. We saw a Japan only recently risen from the ashes of humiliating defeat, energetically rebuilding itself in the American rather than the European image.

Physically, the Japan we saw was not essentially different from the land that had so enchanted my father, especially in the historic Yamato region that had been mercifully left untouched by war. Kyoto was larger and more populous. Some of its buildings were higher. Its hotels were air-conditioned, westernized and more luxurious. Instead of rough gravel roads over which one bumped in swaying rickshas, there were paved highways along which automobiles traveled at often frightening speed. The countryside was essentially unchanged —green mountains, narrow valleys neatly partitioned into rice paddies, tea plantations and truck gardens, blue lakes, tidy little houses and, here and there, hills crowned by shrines and pagodas.

Most of Japan's cities—Tokyo, Osaka, Yokohama, Kobe, Nagoya, Nagasaki and Hiroshima—had been all but obliterated by American bombs in 1945. All of them had been rebuilt and were now vastly larger than they had been in 1893. To a very large extent they had lost their Japanese character, although some of the ancient landmarks had been carefully restored or rebuilt. Except for the Japanese billboards and the very interesting development of underground shopping and amusement centers, the cities of Japan might easily have been American cities—not European, because, in most European towns and cities, one is still conscious of the past. It is not that the Japanese have copied American cities; indeed, in some respects they have improved upon them, especially in rapid transit facilities; it is just that complete rebuilding has resulted in the kind of modernization of which the United States has been the chief exponent. Overcrowding and urban sprawl have created much the same problems from which American cities suffer, except that there are no old-established ethnic ghettos. Tokyo, Osaka, Kobe and Yokohama are architecturally as raw as the cities of Texas; only a few carefully preserved remnants of the past and the little green islands of beautifully landscaped parks and gardens give urban Japan an authentic Japanese character.

We made a pilgrimage of penance to Hiroshima, where some two hundred thousand people were killed or horribly maimed in the flash of the first atomic bomb. I wish all Americans could have this experience. The city was completely wiped out except for the mutilated skeletons of a few concrete and steel structures, one of which has been left standing. Hiroshima has now been rebuilt and looks much like any number of American cities, except for the Peace Park and its haunting museum of horrors. Blown-up photographs of dead and dying men, women and children, their clothes burned off or fused to their tortured bodies—a child with no face—a woman with her breasts covered with a nauseating crust—the shadow of a man whose body no longer exists—molten fragments of wood fused to stone—the charred remnants of a few pitiful belongings . . .

We were the only Americans among numerous Japanese wandering through this grisly reminder of man's inhumanity to man—of *our* inhumanity toward the very people who were walking beside us. They gave no sign of recognizing us as Americans, no sign of hostility. We felt sick and ashamed— ashamed not of being Americans but of being part of a human species capable of greater cruelty than the animals.

Our English-speaking guide, Hirobumi Takahashi, who accompanied us throughout our stay in Japan, told us that there was very little resentment in Japan over the atom-bombing of Hiroshima and Nagasaki. Most Japanese, he said, felt that the two atom bombs had shortened the war, thus saving more lives than they destroyed. I asked him how long Japan could have held out if the war had gone on. "Two months," he said, "maybe until November." Agreeing with him that many more Japanese and Americans would have been killed if the American forces had invaded Honshu or Kyushu, I asked, "What would have happened if the Americans had not invaded—if they had simply kept up their blockade and waited?" This seemed to be a possibility he had not considered. After a pause he said:

"In that case, we would have had to surrender in a few months. We had nothing left. No fuel for our few remaining planes. No iron or steel . . . all the iron railings on bridges and buildings had already been melted down to make steel . . . we were cut off from Manchuria. . . . Food was so scarce that I traded my fine German piano for four bushels of rice to feed my four children, and there were others worse off than I. . . ."

"Then why," I said, "do people think the bombs ended the war? Why did they save more lives than they destroyed?"

169

"They made it possible," he said, "for the emperor to order surrender. The emperor wanted peace . . . he never wanted war . . . but he could not act until the bombs fell because all the people had been told, even as late as August, that we were winning." And then, after a pause, he added: "Even I, who had not wanted the war, cried when I heard the emperor's order to surrender. I had not wanted the war but I did not want Japan to lose it."

Takahashi—Taki, we called him at his request—was the descendant of an old samurai family. (He was not related to the former finance minister whom my father had known.) One of his ancestors had perhaps been a *ronin*, a samurai who lost his overlord. In any case, Taki was extremely well educated and knew every detail of his country's history. In addition, he was a fine horseman, a skilled fencer and a good shot with bow and arrow. He had been taught horsemanship by the nephew of Count Kentaro Kaneko, a friend of President Theodore Roosevelt. In the army, Taki had wangled himself a noncombatant job. After the surrender he had been one of General MacArthur's interpreters. Unsuccessful in business, he had become an outstandingly excellent guide. As we wandered through Japan, Taki poured out history, often well spiced with legend and anecdote. We visited his house and met his pretty wife, whom he introduced in true Japanese style as "my stupid wife." (Denigrating one's family and possessions is one of the many forms of Japanese politeness. The Japanese are easily embarrassed and dread embarrassing a friend as much as they dread being themselves embarrassed. Hence the giving or receiving of gifts is a delicate matter. Tips are not given or expected, except in very rare cases; if offered, they are usually politely declined. Too many Americans are beginning to spoil this pleasant custom.)

The reward of the penitent pilgrim to Hiroshima is a visit

to the lovely sacred island of Miyajima, a short drive and then a ferry ride across an arm of the Inland Sea. From the landing one walks about half a mile along the single, tourist-trapped little village street until one comes to the beautiful floating red temple of Itsukushima, built in Chinese Buddhist style in 806. Above the floating shrine a five-story pagoda stands upon a little hill. The place swarms with Japanese tourists, but no one is permitted to be born or to die on the island. The shrine is one of two that every Japanese hopes to visit at least once during his lifetime. (The other is the beautiful Shinto Ise shrine near Toba which is moved once every twenty years to a new location among its giant cryptomeria trees.)

Speaking of Toba, this is the home of the famous Mikimoto cultured pearl—an item which did not exist in my father's day and which I am sure he would have resented, because it destroyed the rarity value of one of nature's most exquisite products. The story of Mr. Mikimoto is of interest.

He began life as a humble noodle merchant who wanted very much to go to Paradise. In preparing for his own funeral, he dropped in at a jewelry store and there learned how pearls were formed in oysters by the accidental intrusion of a grain of sand or other foreign matter. He studied the life of oysters and found that they changed sex every year; and that a three-year-old female oyster was most susceptible to the introduction of an irritant which would in time form a pearl. He and his wife then invented the extremely complicated process of injecting a bit of mussel shell into three-year-old lady oysters, changing them from salt to fresh water and finally hanging them in cages to mature, once more in salt water. At Toba, one sees the whole six-year process from beginning to end. To attract tourists, there is a much-advertised show of girl pearl divers that illustrates how pearls were originally (and, I think, more attractively) gathered. The "girls," however, are women and not, as subtly suggested in the advertisements, half-naked; they wear extremely modest white-skirted bathing dresses. A visit to Toba, two hours away from Kyoto by car, is not a "must" for those interested in Japan.

Another modern tourist trap, visited by thousands of Japanese as well as by foreigners, is the "Opera" at Tarakazuka, near Kobe. The theater, along with a small zoo, was built by the chief shareholder in one of Japan's privately owned smaller railroads. The line was not making money and so the energetic part-owner developed the little resort town of Tarakazuka into an amusement center. He now has a gold mine. The "Opera" itself is a revue, the first part of which presents abbreviated versions of a Noh drama and a Kabuki play, while the second half offers a modern musical play followed by a parody of American comedy. This too may well be omitted from one's itinerary, especially if one is going to see a real Noh drama and a real Kabuki play in Tokyo.

Far more rewarding is a trip from Kobe across the Inland Sea to the town of Takamatsu, situated on the island of Shikoku, the smallest of the four main islands. The little white ships that ply the Inland Sea between Kobe and Beppu, on Kyushu, are beautifully fitted out with cabins, lounges, saloon and snack bar. We were fortunate in having clear, sunny weather and could fully enjoy the succession of oddly shaped islands that stud this marine fairyland. All these islands are covered with green vegetation. Some are inhabited only by monkeys; on others there are little villages and harbors that were once the haunts of pirates. Wedge-shaped salt-extraction fields can be seen on a few of the larger islands. Little fishing boats with square sails shine in the sun. Occasionally one sees a sea-going freighter or an oil tanker. All this ever-changing scene passes before one's eyes while a juke box blares American jazz and a television set, showing a game of baseball in progress, competes with the juke box. (The Japanese do not seem to mind noise and are especially partial to American rock-and-roll. They are also rabid baseball fans.) The ship is crowded with gay Japanese families sightseeing in their own country. Our friend Taki had to shout to make himself heard as he pointed out the hill near Takamatsu which we were to climb the next day in order to visit the scene of one of the last great battles between the Heike and Genji clans, fought in 1184–1185. Taki was delighted to discover that I had already told my family about the battle of Yashima Plain, the victory of the Genji and the establishment of the Bakufu government at Kamakura. He corrected me when I attributed the victory to Yoritomo, who became the first shogun, and informed us that it was Yoritomo's brother, Yoshitsune, who triumphed at Yashima. As we entered the little harbor of Takamatsu, Taki promised to tell us an interesting story about Yoshitsune after dinner at the hotel. (The story turned out to be the legend, referred to in a previous chapter, according to which Yoshitsune, whose name in Chinese was Gengi Kei, escaped from his jealous brother's pursuit and fled to Mongolia, where he became the famous Mongol conqueror, Genghis Khan.)

The path up to the battlefield on Yashima Hill is steep. At its entrance we found several palanquins and their bearers, waiting to carry visitors too lazy, too old or too feeble to climb the hill. Much to our children's delight, Taki insisted that I ride in one of these contraptions. "After all," he said, "you told me that your father often traveled this way in Japan. People will think that you are a very important person." Somewhat embarrassed, I climbed in. Two sturdy little Japanese shouldered the bamboo pole and trotted off with me. Not only my family but a number of laughing Japanese took pictures. It was highly amusing to everyone but me.

There was not very much to see at the site of the battle. A Shinto shrine stood near the crest of the hill. Further up there were little booths offering souvenirs and the ubiquitous Coca-Cola. Young and old bought little clay saucers to compete in scaling them as far as possible down the steep hillside. The view of the sparkling Inland Sea was reward enough, especially for one who had arrived at the top without moving a muscle.

Another interesting bit of history from Taki:

So-called battles in the old days were often actually fought only by personal combat between two opposing leaders. Apparently they would come forward from their respective troops, stand facing each other and begin to hurl insults, each with the object of making the other lose his temper. To lose one's temper frequently meant losing the advantage and one's life. Sometimes, Taki said, generals would use stand-ins to do the fighting. People who believe the Yoshitsune-Genghis legend say that Yoshitsune was not killed at Yashima Hill as history records, because he used such a stand-in. I think Taki half-believed the legend himself; and, indeed, it is tempting for any Japanese to believe that the great Mongol conqueror was actually a native of Japan.

One thing that I wish my father had seen and described was the cormorant-fishing at Gifu, a town not very far from Nagoya. (Perhaps it was *too* far in his day. It took us almost three hours in an automobile.)

We had spent a long and rather tiring morning in Nagoya visiting porcelain and cloisonné factories and somewhat wearily set out for Gifu in the afternoon, arriving there at about six o'clock. After dinner at a riverside hotel, we hired one of the hundreds of fifteen-foot canopied boats moored along the bank or already lined up along the opposite shore side by side. On each boat under the canopy there was a tatami mat, a long table between two long benches over which hung a paper lantern. Leaving our shoes at the unmatted end of the boat, we crawled under the low canopy and sat down, while our boatman proceeded to pole our craft across the river to join the fast-thickening cluster of similar vessels. Soon we were in place between two other boats, on each of which gay groups of Japanese were eating their supper chattering merrily. It was growing dark and one could sense an air of anticipation. One by one the paper lanterns were lit and, as more and more boats collected, the river took on a festive appearance. Presently a slightly larger boat came downstream with a little band playing and six geisha girls going through the slow, stately movements of a dance. A woman in a small rowboat came along selling fireworks. Almost every group bought Roman candles and whirligigs. Pretty soon the whole river was lit up with colored lights and whirling pinwheels of fire. Two pretty girls in the boat beside ours sang us some Japanese songs. From boat to boat, people chatted and offered each other drinks. . . .

And now it grew really dark. The stars were suddenly out and a gibbous moon rose over the mountain behind us. A sort of happy tension mounted. The geisha boat passed again with the girls singing. People had used up their fireworks and were now almost all straining their eyes upstream. Suddenly there was a shout far away on our right. Taki said, "Here they come!"

About half a mile upstream we could see a flaming torch, then another and another, quickly coming nearer. Soon we could dimly see that there were three boats with a man holding aloft a torch at the bow of each. As they came rapidly nearer, we could see that each boat held two other figures, one seated at the feet of the torch bearer, the other erect at the stern. And then we could see that the seated figure held a lot of thin ropes in his hands. As the three boats flashed by, we saw that each was preceded by a dozen or so rapidly swimming birds with long black heads and necks, each of them apparently attached to one of the thin lines, so that one momentarily had the illusion of seeing a man handling a team of many waterfowl that were pulling his boat downstream at tremendous speed. As the last boat went by, one could see that some of these birds were diving, and then, in the suddenly bright illumination of the flaming torch, we saw a cormorant pulled out of the water and a fish taken from his open beak by the handler. (Taki told us that the birds have rings around their necks which prevent their swallowing. Our youngest girl thought this was cruel, but Taki reassured her that, after they had done their work, the birds would be well fed.)

Scarcely had the three fishing boats passed when three more appeared. By this time we knew where to look and could see the cormorants diving and being pulled aboard to deliver their catch. Then another group of three, and still another, until the last boat passed and the show was over—but not really over. For now all the spectator boats broke out of their orderly line-up and rushed—their boatmen poling, pushing each other and shouting—downstream to where the cormorant boats were idly drifting, with the flames of their torches slowly dying, their crews resting and the birds being fed. Reluctantly we went ashore and back to Nagoya. We had seen a bit of the old Japan that none of us would ever forget.

We had hoped to learn a little about what the people of present-day Japan were thinking and what part they might be expected to play in world affairs. But time was too short. We did, however, learn quite a little from carefully reading the excellent English-language press, particularly its coverage and comments upon a top-level conference of Japanese and American officials, held in Kyoto while we were in Japan, and the editorial welcome extended to Soviet Foreign Minister Gromyko during his brief visit. It was the first such visit to Japan since the war. During our weeks in Japan, United States Ambassador Reischauer announced his retirement after over five years of service in Tokyo, causing an avalanche of editorials regretting his departure and uniformly praising his and his wife's successful efforts to reopen a friendly dialogue between not only the governments but the people of Japan and the United States. Rarely has the United States chosen an ambassador more ideally suited to his post.

Everything we learned confirmed the impression that Japan has reached the point at which it is cautiously beginning to look outward and to develop an independent foreign policy both with respect to the Soviet Union and with respect to China. The Japanese are irked by the political restrictions imposed upon them by their military and economic dependence upon the United States. (The United States is Japan's largest customer.) They are irked particularly by the fact that Washington frowns upon their doing business with China, although I think they perhaps overestimate how much trade they could develop with that country at the present time. (China's meager export earnings are, for the time being, pre-empted by its need to import foreign foodstuffs, especially wheat, which Japan cannot supply.) On the other hand, Japan could supply, and the Soviet Union now apparently wants, help in the economic development of Siberia. This is a new twist which might well be encouraged by Washington.

The American occupation of Okinawa and its use as a rear base in the Vietnamese war is another irritant. Premier Eisaku Sato, like his able predecessor, Hayato Ikeda, loyally defends American policy in Asia but some of the press is out-

177

spoken in its criticism of our intervention in Vietnam and of our intransigence toward China. This is true of such influential newspapers as the *Japan Times, Yomiuri, Mainichi* and others normally friendly to the United States. Our action in Korea was supported in Japan, first of all because it seemed right and was backed by the United Nations, and second, because it gave a great stimulus to the Japanese economy. Our action in Vietnam is unpopular because it seems to many Japanese neither morally nor pragmatically justified, because it has become a white man's war against Asians, and because it threatens Asian and world peace. Given internal political stability, it would not be surprising if the Japanese government were to make a strong effort to bring about an end to the conflict.

As for internal political stability, in the summer of 1966 the conservative-minded Liberal Democratic Party seemed well ensconced in power in spite of a certain number of scandals. The Socialist opposition lacked unity and appeared unlikely to register any substantial gains in the next general election. The unknown factor, about which it was difficult to obtain information, was the new but rapidly growing Komitei (Clean Government) Party, which had been formed as the political arm of a modernized Nichiren-Zen Buddhist movement, known as Soka Gakkai. This movement, so far as we could learn a mixture of revivalism, nationalism and neutralism, appeared to be gaining a large following among the lower middle class. The Komitei had achieved considerable success in some local elections and was expected to run candidates for the Diet. What the party's impact would be was the subject of much speculation.*

* The elections of January 1967 gave Premier Sato and his Liberal Democratic Party a solid majority, with the Socialists weakened by a split between the pro and anti-Chinese factions. The Komitei ran thirty-two candi-

In his farewell remarks, Ambassador Reischauer predicted that the future of Asia would depend more upon Japan than upon China. To which one might add the impression that the more independent Tokyo makes itself of Washington's Asian policy, the stronger will be its influence.

At the people-to-people level, the Japanese show a very real friendliness toward the United States, due largely, I think, to the behavior of American troops and civilians during the occupation. Knowing what their own troops had done in China, the Japanese must have expected the worst, much as the Germans expected the worst from their Russian conquerors. However, unlike the Germans, the Japanese faced their guilt and made few if any excuses for their wrongdoing, appreciated generous treatment and cooperated enthusiastically with the occupiers. And, unlike the Germans, they are not given to self-pity or complaint against their friends. This much even the most casual observer can see—which does not mean that he has gained any insight into the complicated and somewhat inscrutable nature of the Japanese people.

To my surprise, I found myself more attracted to the old Japan than to the new. The old Japan seemed somehow familiar, though I had known it only from books. In spite of its Americanization, the new Japan seemed curiously more difficult to understand and appreciate. I am not sure that Americanization, or westernization, has been an unmixed blessing for the Japanese people, except in a purely material sense. One admires Japan's progress in the industrial field, where, only a short time ago, Japanese manufacturers were exploiting cheap labor, pirating designs and flooding the world with shoddy products, and where now Japan makes better and cheaper

---

dates for seats in the Diet and succeeded in electing twenty-one. It remains to be seen whether this is merely a flash in the pan or the beginning of a powerful and somewhat unpredictable movement.

cameras than Germany and competes successfully in electronics with leading American manufacturers. And it is not only in light industry that Japan has made astonishing progress. Japanese shipyards are outbuilding those of Britain and Germany. Japan's railroads are among the best, if not actually the finest, in the world. Japanese automobiles are finding their way into world markets. And yet one feels that something has been lost; it is hard to say just what; certainly it is not the "quaintness" so highly touted in travel-bureau literature. What has been lost—if, indeed, anything has been lost—is something of the spirit, of the quiet contemplation of nature and the slow pace of life in the old Japan. Perhaps this is what modernization does to all peoples. . . .

One wonders what would have happened if Japan's doors had not been forced open. To be sure, Japan was not raped by the West, as was China. But its latticed windows were forced open at a time when exposure to Western "civilization" meant exposure to the contagion of mercantile greed and ruthless competitive imperialism. I left Japan with something of the same feeling with which I had left Hong Kong—a feeling that the East might have been better off without the advent of Western Man.

Supposedly the West's great gift to the East was the idea of progress—the knowledge that fate is not immutable and that man is the master of his own destiny. But who is to say that, in their own time and in their own way, the Eastern peoples would not have discovered this for themselves and thus found their own way into the modern world?

Our Fiftieth State

Coming from the Far East to Hawaii, one's first impression, influenced perhaps by one's knowledge of Hawaii's history, is that here is another example of what the Western intrusion has done to the East. Honolulu is fast becoming a second Miami Beach, with mainland tourists overcrowding its beaches, bars, restaurants, neon-lit movie theaters and luxury hotels. Even the beautiful Outer Islands are being invaded by real estate developers and builders of "destination complexes" for tourists, each with its hotels, golf courses and supermarkets. Gone is the old Hawaii where Robert Louis Stevenson wrote under his favorite banyan tree and about which Mark Twain declared: "No other land in all the world has any deep, strong charms for me but that one; no other land could so longingly and beseechingly haunt me, sleeping and waking, through half a lifetime. . . ."

The old Hawaii is gone, and before one has penetrated beneath the outer unattractive layer of the new Hawaii, one is tempted to draw a wrong conclusion; namely, that because the history of Hawaii's annexation is sordid and disreputable, the result must inevitably be discreditable.

One might expect to find among the present-day Hawaiians at least some residue of resentment, and perhaps it does exist in some of the few old Hawaiian families, but the only mildly hostile recollection one now encounters is directed not at the American planters and business interests but at the early missionaries who insisted that hula dancers wear Mother Hubbards and introduced Puritan prudery among a carefree and innocent people.

Far from realizing the expectation that disreputable history would produce a lamentable result, one's first disagreeable impression of present-day Hawaii as being nothing much more than a tourist haven is soon dispelled. It *is* a tourist haven and will probably become even more so. (In 1965 there were over six hundred thousand visitors, about one third of them from the United States and the remainder mostly from Canada, Japan, Australia and New Zealand. The further development of air travel is almost certain to increase the numbers of people who visit the islands.) But this is only one aspect of the Hawaii of today. The fiftieth state of our Union has developed a multiracial society which is in many respects a model of what one hopes the future world may be.

The population of the Hawaiian Islands is about 750,000, composed of 39 percent Caucasian, 28 percent Japanese, 14 percent part-Hawaiian, 10 percent Filipino, 5 percent Chinese, 1 percent Negro and 1 percent pure Hawaiian. Among those listed as Caucasian are large numbers of Portuguese and quite a few assorted Europeans. (On one of the islands our guide had a mother half-Chinese and half-Hawaiian and a father half-Czech and half-German. Another guide had an Irish-Chinese mother and a Japanese-Filipino-Hawaiian father.) Questions about ancestry are as a rule welcomed rather than resented. Most Hawaiians are proud of the fact that their society demonstrates the unity of the human race. And, indeed, no other place on this troubled earth so joyously contradicts Rudyard Kipling's assertion that "East is East and West is West and never the twain shall meet." On Hawaii's beautiful islands, East and West have not only met but intermingled and intermarried to form a unique and happy society.

Not only is there no discoverable residue of resentment against the United States, but one finds that present-day Hawaiians are almost fiercely proud of being Americans. A visitor's tactlessly phrased "Have you ever been to the United States?" is likely to be answered: "Sir [or Madam], do you mean have I ever been to the mainland?" We are more readily forgiven for the past than for any present-day failure to recognize that Hawaiians are our fellow citizens. It is significant that of Hawaii's two members of the United States Senate one (the Honorable Hiram J. Fong) is racially Chinese, while the other (the Honorable Daniel Inouye) is of Japanese descent.

Were it not for the widely shared prosperity of the Hawaiian population, there would probably be some resentment over the fact that mainlanders own most of the best land and most of the rapidly developing industries. But the citizens of our fiftieth state enjoy an annual per-capita income of about three thousand dollars, which is above the national average in the United States, and unemployment is no problem.

Hawaii has an excellent school system. We heard that over 160,000 students were enrolled in its 209 public schools. The University of Hawaii is probably the most universal university in the world. At its East-West Center, remarkable work is being done in the study of interracial relations and the physical, biological and psychological factors which make for racial harmony. The center provides invaluable training for members of the Peace Corps and A.I.D. administration. There are also in progress at the university highly significant studies in astronomy and oceanography, for both of which Hawaii is an ideal location. The Space Agency of the Federal Government maintains a number of tracking stations on the islands; the volcanic craters are used to study the probable surface of the moon. Except for the Defense Department's use of rugged Hawaiian terrain for training in guerrilla warfare and certain naval activities, present-day Hawaii can properly be described as a laboratory for studying the creation of a peaceful world.

On the island of Oahu, not very far from Honolulu, the Mormon Church has created a Polynesian Cultural Center comprising authentic Tonga, Tahitian, Fiji, Maori and Hawaiian villages. University students from these Polynesian communities earn their expenses by manning their respective villages, showing visitors how their people live or have lived for unknown centuries. Here one sees how the various tribes build their houses, how they make tapa cloth and rope from the barks of trees, how they construct their outrigger canoes, what implements and weapons they use, and how they prepare the abundant food that nature provides for them. In the evening one can witness the wild and beautiful tribal dances, accompanied by the savage, stirring beat of their drums. This is about the only place on the Hawaiian Islands where one can get some idea of the sort of civilization which has been submerged by the flood of Eastern and Western invaders.

The old Hawaii has vanished. But, no matter how much one may regret the disappearance of the land which so haunted the dreams of Mark Twain and many others—no matter how greatly one may dislike the tawdry overlay of westernization that caters to the whims of affluent pleasure-seekers—one comes away from present-day Hawaii with a deep sense of respect for its multiracial people and with renewed hope for man's future.

It may interest the reader to see the reaction to our pilgrimage of our twelve-year-old son, who kept a diary throughout our trip while his older brother and sister took pictures.

What I Got Out of Our Trip
PHILIP WARBURG

"Our trip to the Orient was a great opportunity for the entire family. Dad's daily lectures on the ship were extremely helpful. They gave us a broad look at the history of the ancient Asian civilizations about which we have learned nothing in school. Some of the things he told us about we saw in Hong Kong and Japan.

"My first impression of Hong Kong was a beautiful city at the foot of majestic mountains. Later I discovered that it was not quite so beautiful. It is impossible for me to describe how shocked I was by the poverty of so many people. Some of them were just skin and bones. Many were sprawled all over the dirty streets, too weak to move. This was mostly in the New Territories. These poor souls are just a small percentage of the many millions of poverty-stricken people in Asia. One thing that is difficult to understand is that they don't seem to realize how poor they are and seem perfectly satisfied with what little they have. Some of them live on tiny boats, called sampans; the bigger ones are called junks. On the Hakka farms the women do all the work; the men go away to find jobs. Many families in Hong Kong live in horrible run-down shantytowns. Before Hong Kong, I thought that the slums in New York City were as bad as they come, but to the poor people of Hong Kong the New York slums would seem like the height of luxury. There is a drastic difference between the wealthy foreigners and Chinese living in Hong Kong and the poor people.

"One of the many things I learned from our visit to Hong Kong was to be ever so grateful for how fortunate we and all Americans are. When we came back to the luxurious Peninsula Hotel, I felt guilty to be living in such beautiful rooms with clothes to wear and plenty of food to eat. . . .

"Before our visit to Japan, I had pictured it as being a picturesque country with nothing but Japanese-style buildings, kimonos and public bathtubs. I found it to be much different. The cities in Japan were all very modern and Americanized. One had to go out into the country to see what Japan was really like. Tokyo was another New York except with Japa-

185

nese street signs. The Japanese people are very friendly. Twenty years ago we bombed Hiroshima and killed many thousands of Japanese people. Much to my surprise, instead of holding all Americans in contempt, the Japanese respect Americans. The reason they do is that the United States was the first nation to help a country it had conquered to get a good start on rebuilding and re-establishing itself. The unnecessary bombing of Hiroshima is an example of why war should be abolished. I was amazed at how many Japanese could speak English. Whenever possible, I tried to make conversation with Japanese people. A great deal of the time I found that they could speak English. I think that this just proves how ignorant we are. We wouldn't think of learning Japanese, or any other Asian tongue. Until this year at school (seventh grade) we were taught only English. English is a major subject in Japanese schools, starting in very low grades. One thing that I regret is that we did not visit a Japanese school. It would have been interesting to see how the classes were conducted.

"The Japanese are very generous. It is their custom to give presents to any guest that comes to their house. They go overboard in this respect. One can't pay a compliment about some object without the owner insisting that one take it. There are many other strange Japanese customs and rituals. A man must always say bad things about his family. When we visited a Japanese home, our host introduced his wife as 'my miserable wife' and his son as 'my stupid sucking pig.' His dog's name was 'Stupid.' These absurdities are considered politeness. . . .

"Hawaii is a vacationer's paradise. The Hawaiians are very friendly, restful people. There are not many pure Hawaiians left. Many of them have crossbred with people of other nationalities. There are many Japanese, Chinese, Portuguese, Spanish, Irish and English living in Hawaii. If all countries cross-bred as Hawaiians do, there wouldn't be anywhere near as much conflict and wars between nations because they would be more *united*. I think it would be wonderful if that were someday to happen.

"I did not see one thin Hawaiian. They all get fat from eating poi, a vegetable that is eaten with the fingers and tastes like wallpaper paste.

"We surfed a great deal. It was lots of fun.

"The Hawaiian islands were formed by volcanoes. There are still many craters and we saw one that was smoking a great deal.

"What I enjoyed most on our trip was learning about the places we visited. I kept a daily diary describing everything we saw and heard. Our trip gave me the desire to learn more and to widen my knowledge of Asia."

10

Imperialism and Anticolonialism

I

THE AMERICAN
ILLUSION OF INNOCENCE

Many of us cherish the belief that our country has been the consistent champion of national independence and self-determination. The belief springs from the fact that our ancestors in the thirteen colonies broke the path to freedom from colonial rule and that their example was followed by the leaders of Latin American revolt against Spanish and Portuguese rule. But the history we have traced shows that the nineteenth-century behavior of the United States toward weaker nations and peoples closely resembled that of the European powers during that age of colonial empire-building.

The European nations, large in terms of population and small in area, shared a continent in which there was little room to expand. Unable or unwilling to cooperate with each

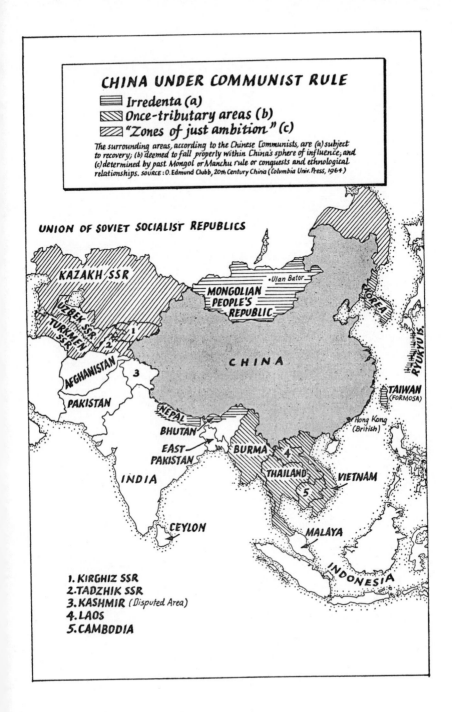

other and jealous of their individual sovereignties, they competed fiercely, at first within the narrow confines of Europe, then in overseas trade and finally in the acquisition of overseas possessions. Our forefathers, on the other hand, acquired a vast, rich and sparsely settled continent by wars and broken treaties with the aborigines, by purchase from the European powers and finally by an imperialistic war against Mexico.

Once the United States had reached the shores of the Pacific, it had no rational need to expand farther. Yet this was precisely the point at which the American people embarked upon overseas expansion, motivated by much the same mercantile hunger for profit, much the same missionary zeal and eventually much the same desire to possess and exploit the natural resources of foreign lands as had impelled the European powers into the Americas, Asia and Africa.

The purchase of Alaska in 1867 had served two legitimate strategic purposes: it eliminated Russia from the North American continent and forestalled a possible British purchase of Alaska. Similarly, in a world of predatory powers, there was reason to fear that Britain or Japan might annex the Hawaiian Islands. But, if national security had been the primary concern of the United States, this could have been assured by a hands-off declaration similar to the Monroe Doctrine. As we have seen, however, the annexation of Hawaii came about primarily from a typical nineteenth-century drive to exploit, "civilize" and ultimately to possess in order to protect the private exploiters and self-appointed "civilizers."

There is a saying in Hawaii that "the missionaries came to do good and did well." And it is true that missionary blood flows in the veins of many of the wealthy Hawaiian descendants of planters and traders. But it is also true that, if some of the missionaries "did well" for themselves, they "did good" in more ways than in bringing Christianity to the carefree pagan

191

people of the islands. (Unfortunately they and the traders also brought measles and other diseases which all but wiped out the native population.) One might well ask two broader questions, relating not merely to one particular group of "civilizers" in one particular country but to *"la mission civilizatrice"* of Western Man as a whole. By what right was Western Man entitled to assume that his civilization was superior to all others—not merely superior to the primitive tribal cultures in some parts of the world, but to the highly developed ancient civilization of Asia? And by what right did Western Man assert that his Christian religion offered the sole road to salvation? I shall not attempt to answer these questions, but they deserve at least to be raised.

Whether or not there was in fact any moral or altruistic justification for the West's intrusion upon the East, it cannot be denied that the United States injected itself into Europe's game of competitive imperialism, adopting both Europe's predatory mercantilism and its messianic rationalizations. At first the American quest for trade advantage and missionary zeal led only to participation in the concessions wrung by the European powers from China, including participation in the privileges acquired under the "unequal treaties." Then the same doctrine was applied to Japan, this time with the United States taking the initiative. And finally, toward the end of the century, the American people, bemused by the delusion of their "manifest destiny" to move westward across the Pacific, joined in the quest for outright colonial possessions.

From 1898 until the outbreak of World War I, American diplomacy was just as imperialistic as that of Britain, France, Germany, Russia and Japan, except that it was somewhat less intelligent. And, from 1919 to 1933, American diplomacy in the Far East was—to say the least—counterproductive in that

192

it endangered rather than protected the American stake in the Far East.

The fact is that the anticolonialism upon which some of us pride ourselves today is a myth. American anticolonialism existed in the early days of the nation and then all but died, coming to life again only during the first administration of Franklin D. Roosevelt. In his first inaugural address Roosevelt declared: "In the field of world policy I would dedicate this nation to the policy of the good neighbor, the neighbor who resolutely respects himself and, because he does so, respects the rights of others."

A number of actions followed this declaration; the renunciation of armed intervention in Latin America (1933); the abrogation of the Platt Amendment with respect to Cuba (1934); the withdrawal of Marines from Haiti (1934); the multilateralization of the Monroe Doctrine (1936); and the granting of Philippine independence in 1946 in accordance with the Tydings-McDuffie Act of 1935. Toward the end of World War II, Roosevelt proposed that France's former colonial possessions in Indochina be placed under United Nations trusteeship and urged a reluctant Britain to free India.

This reawakening of the early American spirit did not last long. Under Roosevelt's successors, the United States became so obsessed with anticommunism that it allied itself with any and all anticommunist governments—native or colonial, democratic or totalitarian. Under Presidents Truman and Eisenhower, the United States became a status quo power, afraid of change anywhere in the world for fear that change might lead to "Godless communism." In appointing itself the global guardian against communism, the United States lost touch with the rising tide of nationalism and, by failure to befriend nationalism, became its enemy, allowing the two great com-

193

munist powers to identify with the emerging peoples and to assume a spurious role as their protectors. Then, in order to compete with the communist powers for the allegiance of the emerging peoples, the United States began to urge its European Cold War allies to accelerate the pace of decolonization. Partly as a result of this prodding and partly because of the impatience of the peoples seeking independence, decolonization proceeded in some cases, notably in Africa, too fast and with insufficient preparation. Thus anti-American sentiment grew both among the old colonial powers and the peoples seeking independence; the European powers resented American prodding, while the emerging peoples in Africa and Asia considered the United States a status quo defender or—worse —a neocolonialist power.

The twentieth-century anticolonial revolution began in Asia, spreading from there to other parts of the world. The ideal role of the United States in the postwar period would have been to aid both the colonial powers and the impatient peoples seeking national independence to proceed with adequate care and preparation. This function the United States has not fulfilled, nor could it have been fulfilled by a nation obsessed with the overriding fear of communism and, because of its obsession, devoting its vast resources to the preservation of a status quo rejected by the majority of mankind.

The truth is that, except for the magnificent period when the founding fathers dedicated their youthful nation to the championship of freedom for "all men everywhere"—except for the brief moment when Abraham Lincoln rose on the floor of the Congress to denounce the imperialist war against Mexico—and except for the years when Franklin D. Rossevelt inhabited the White House—the United States has not been an antiimperialist power.

II

UNINTENTIONAL
AMERICAN NEOCOLONIALISM

Ever since 1947 the United States has been a well-intentioned, self-appointed arbiter of what should or should not happen in the emerging nations. It has acted upon the assumption that what is good for the United States is good for the world. It has tried to sell free-enterprise capitalism to young nations in which there was no indigenous private capital, to sell parliamentary democracy to peoples with no experience in representative self-government, and to defend freedom where no freedom in the Western sense had ever existed. This has been a form of well-meaning but unwise neocolonialism born of no selfish motive other than the obsessive fear of communism—a motivation incomprehensible to most of the formerly dependent peoples. In dealing with these peoples the United States has tried to apply to them the almost wholly irrelevent experience gained in halting communist expansion into western Europe, forgetting that there it had dealt with a group of old, long-industrialized nations with highly trained administrative bureaucracies, a long tradition of democracy and an inherent dislike of communism born of years of successful capitalist development. The United States did not tell Europe what to do; it merely helped Europe to do what the majority of western Europeans already wanted to do. This was not neocolonialism, even though the preponderant military and economic power of the United States tended to reduce western Europe to semidependence against which it is now in revolt.

In Asia, on the other hand, the United States has behaved since 1947 rather like Victorian Britain in the nineteenth century, although for wholly different reasons. Nineteenth-century Britain acted to expand the British Empire and to hold world dominance by preserving a balance of power in which Britain could throw its decisive weight against any nation or group of nations that might challenge British supremacy. This was frank imperialism, disliked but understood by the Asian peoples.

The United States has intervened in Asia during the postwar period not because it sought domination but because it decided, for itself and for others, that Asia must not be allowed to "go communist." Thus motivated, the United States intervened in the Chinese civil war and, after its intervention failed to halt communism, proceeded to encircle the Chinese mainland with sea power, military bases and alliances contracted with any and all Asian governments that declared their anti-communism. Unfortunately, most of these governments were dominated by antidemocratic ruling cliques, unresponsive to the needs and aspirations of the majority of their peoples. By allying itself with them, the United States alienated both nationalism and the "revolution of rising expectation."

The tragedy of Vietnam illustrates what happens when a foreign power—be it France or the United States—suppresses nationalist revolution and allies itself with a corrupt and selfish mandarin clique, thus literally driving the revolutionary nationalist movement into the arms of the communists.

On the other hand, what has happened in Indonesia since it became independent is instructive. Here the United States vacillated, first supporting the Dutch colonial power and then switching its support to the nationalist movement, thus more or less neutralizing its influence upon developments. And here, the communist powers were the foreign interventionists who sought to capture the nationalist movement. At first it was the

Soviet Union that tried to draw Indonesia into the communist orbit; then, as the Sino-Soviet split developed, China took over as the intervening communist power. Wisely, the United States refrained from any serious counterintervention, with the result that the Indonesians themselves eventually staged an anti-communist revolution. What happened in Indonesia shows that the drive for national independence and for better living conditions is far stronger in Asia than any ideology— that intervention by a communist power is just as likely to backfire as is "capitalist-imperialist" intervention.

The history of India's postwar foreign relations is equally instructive. Here was a young nation of over four hundred million people struggling to preserve and develop a democratic form of government inherited from the colonial power and, at the same time, endeavoring to create a mixed economy with sectors of public and private enterprise—an economy capable of meeting the vast needs of an impoverished people. No other country in the postwar world was in greater need of foreign aid. No other country was as able to give India such aid as the United States. But, in those early postwar days, the American people looked upon any degree of socialism—i.e., state capitalism—as a step on the road to communism. And when India chose to seek aid from Moscow as well as from Washington, refusing to take sides in the Cold War, Secretary of State Dulles denounced her "neutralism" as "immoral" and refused to extend India any assistance. Instead, Dulles turned to neighboring Pakistan which, chiefly in order to obtain American aid in strengthening itself vis-à-vis India, eagerly declared its willingness to become an anti-communist ally in the Cold War crusade. American rearming of Pakistan forced India to divert a substantial proportion of her meager resources from economic development to countervailing rearmament.

During this early postwar period, India's relations with China were far more friendly than its relations with the United States. India supported Peking's admission to the United Nations. It was through India that China warned the United States against driving through North Korea to the Manchurian border. But soon Chinese-Indian friendship was cooled by China's brutal suppression of a revolt in Tibet; and in 1962 a total break was caused when China entered upon a flirtation with supposedly anti-communist Pakistan and then took advantage of India's preoccupation with a renewed Pakistani threat to Kashmir to send Chinese troops into disputed border territory. Even though the Chinese troops advanced no further and were later withdrawn, these hostile actions shocked India profoundly, causing her to appeal to both Moscow and Washington for military assistance. Both nations responded. To all intents and purposes, China's aggressive actions ended India's "nonalignment" so far as the Far East was concerned, although it did not throw India into the Western camp in opposition to the Soviet Union.

What did this aggressive Chinese behavior accomplish?

1. By humiliating India it alienated a hitherto friendly nation, causing it to improve its relations with China's two major enemies—the "capitalist-imperialist" United States and the communist "revisionist" Soviet Union.

2. It strengthened the hand of the Soviet Union in Asia, enabling it to intervene as the peacemaker when, a few years later, India and Pakistan once more went to war over Kashmir, each using arms supplied by the United States.

3. It caused the United States to adopt a more friendly and more constructive attitude toward India and, equally important, to realize that it had a common interest with the Soviet Union in containing China. (Unhappily, American escalation of the war in Vietnam blocked the development of this com-

mon interest.) Thus, to a very large extent, China's imperialist policy helped the United States to recover from the mistakes of the Dulles era. China's interventionist policies in Asia have alienated about 550 million people in India and Indonesia, almost as many Asian people as the United States has alienated by its interventionist policy in China and Vietnam. This has left Japan, with its hundred million inhabitants and its even more important economic strength, holding the swing position as to Asia's future.

Fortunately Japan is the one important country in Asia in regard to which the United States has made few mistakes during the postwar period. Japan is the one country which has received generous and, on the whole, intelligent American aid. The United States has to a large extent helped the Japanese people to do what they themselves wanted to do; that is, to discover a democratic alternative both to Japan's own past totalitarianism and to Chinese or Soviet-style communism. It has helped the Japanese people to rebuild a prosperous and— so far at least—peace-loving nation.

If the United States has been capable of generous and, on the whole, intelligent treatment of a defeated enemy, why, one must ask, has it preserved an implacable hostility toward China, its former ally in the war against a Japan bent upon conquest? Is it because China intervened in Korea when its Manchurian border was threatened and inflicted a painful defeat upon an American army? Was China really the aggressor in Korea? Was President Eisenhower right when, shortly after the Korean War, he refused to have anything to do with the People's Republic of China because, he said, its people's hands were "dripping with the blood of American boys"? What about Japanese or German hands? What nation's hands have not dripped with blood after a war?

Clearly, Korea is not the real reason for the implacable hos-

199

tility of the United States toward the Chinese People's Republic. The real reason is quite simply that China "went communist"—that the Chinese people committed the unforgivable sin of overthrowing a corrupt, incompetent and tyrannical government, replacing it with a government no less tyrannical but at least more competent and, so far as is known, less corrupt. Yet our own Declaration of Independence, after declaring that "life, liberty and the pursuit of happiness" are the ends for which governments exist, contains these words:

> Whenever any form of government becomes destructive of these ends, it is the right of the people to alter or to abolish it, and to institute a new government, laying its foundation on such principles and organizing its powers in such form as to them shall seem most likely to effect their safety and happiness.

If China today poses a threat to world peace, it is not because China has "gone communist." It is because her leaders fiercely resent not only the treatment they themselves have received since they came to power but also the long list of indignities and injustices from which China has suffered in the past at Western hands; and because these leaders have made the Chinese people as a whole for the first time aware of the past and have taught them to hate those who have inflicted indignity and injustice upon them.

China is dangerous partly just because she is big and powerful, as she would be under any form of government that succeeded in uniting seven hundred million people; but, even more, China is dangerous because she has been frustrated in completing her revolution. Were it not for the United States, the Peking regime would long ago have been recognized by the world as the legitimate government of China, entitled to China's seat in the United Nations and to permanent membership in its Security Council. Had the United States not supported, armed, aided and defended the refugee Nationalist regime on Formosa, that island would long ago have come under Peking's rule as the thirty-fifth province of China. One may doubt whether the seven million natives of Formosa would have welcomed coming under communist rule, but one may also doubt whether they would have chosen to come under the antidemocratic rule of Chiang Kai-shek's Kuomintang refugees. This is not the point; the point is that the Peking regime has been deprived of establishing its rule over an island that both it and the defeated Nationalists consider to be a part of China. Formosa now is to China what the "lost provinces" of Alsace–Lorraine were to France before they were recaptured. (For much the same reason, a truncated and partitioned Germany remains a threat to peace today although, unlike China, West Germany has formally renounced the use of force in seeking to redress what it considers its grievances.)

As long ago as 1954 I ventured to put forward a suggestion for easing tensions in the Far East which at the time found some support in the Congress, although not in the executive branch of our government. Briefly stated, it was this:

> Recognize the Peking regime as the government of China, entitled to occupy China's seat in the United Nations, provided that Peking will agree to placing Formosa under the guardianship of the United Nations pending a free decision by the Formosans as to whether they wish to come under Mainland rule or to establish an independent republic, entitled to separate representation in the world organization.*

* Quoted from Chap. 12, "Preventive Action in Asia," of a short book, *Turning Point Toward Peace*, the full text of which was introduced into the *Congressional Record* by Senator Wayne Morse of Oregon.

At the time when this proposal was put forward it was obvious that neither Mao Tse-tung nor Chiang Kai-shek would accept it, since both insisted, as they still do, that there is only one China, of which Formosa is a part. However, it was pointed out that by advocating such a solution the United States would get into step with the majority of world opinion and gain the respect and support of the Asian peoples, while Peking, should it reject the proposals, would place itself in the role of an aggressor, unwilling to renounce the use of force. Congressman Henry Reuss of Wisconsin, one of those who supported the proposal to put Formosa under United Nations guardianship, put the case succinctly. The United States, he said, "would get out from under the current untenable position whereby we maintain Formosa as a United States province and foist upon it the government of Chiang without the consent of seven million Formosans."

The 1954 proposal raised the basic question: "What should the role of the United States be in Asia and in other parts of the world?" It clearly implied that the United States should *not* act as a self-appointed global anti-communist policeman; that, instead, it should seek to strengthen the United Nations and lend it full support in both peacekeeping and peacemaking. With respect to Formosa, the proposal called for the military neutralization of the island under United Nations guardianship, the demobilization of the Nationalist forces and the withdrawal of American protective power, unless called for by the United Nations, pending a United Nations-supervised plebiscite to determine Formosa's future status.

Over the years there has been sporadic discussion of various versions of what has erroneously been called a "two-Chinas policy." (It is not a question of two Chinas; the question is whether the Peking regime is entitled to China's seat in the

United Nations and, if so, whether Formosa is to become a separate state entitled to its own membership in the United Nations.)

Until the autumn of 1966 the United States inflexibly opposed any alteration of Peking's and Taipei's status and succeeded in blocking all efforts in that direction made at successive sessions of the United Nations General Assembly. Had it not been for Peking's brutality in Tibet, its aggressive attitude toward India in 1962 and the unpredictable outcome of the internal upheaval caused by the "cultural revolution" of 1966, it is very likely that the United States would by this time have been overruled, with the unfortunate result that Peking would probably have been seated without giving any consideration to possible separate Formosan membership.

Early in 1966, before the convulsions of the "cultural revolution" rendered any judgment of China's future course impossible, and when the attitude of our government seemed to be becoming less inflexible, I ventured to put forward a suggestion which might still, some day, aid in a solution of the Formosan problem; namely, that one might recognize that Formosa is, as both sides say, a part of China, but propose that it be given a certain amount of autonomy and separate representation in the United Nations similar to the separate representation of the Ukraine and Byelorussia.* However, until the dust settles in China and the succession to Mao's leadership is determined, it seems unlikely that Peking will consider any proposal for a solution.

As this is written, the whole question of our China policy is overshadowed by the tragic involvement of the United States in a steadily escalating war in Vietnam. My own views as to this matter have been stated in testimony before Congressional

* The idea was put forward in Chap. 10 of *The United States in the Postwar World* (Atheneum, New York, and Gollancz, London, 1966).

committees and in published writings.* They are shared by an increasing number of Americans and need not be repeated here.

Let us, rather, assume that the United States will find an honorable way to terminate its misguided attempt to solve essentially political problems by military means and thus remove one of the major roadblocks to progress toward enduring peace.

What then?

Shall we then recognize the arrogance and folly of what we have been doing in attempting to police the world, undermining instead of strengthening the world organization that we helped to create for that very purpose?

Shall we then recognize that the world does not want and will not accept a *Pax Americana*, no matter how well-intentioned?

Shall we awake from our long ideological nightmare and realize that hunger, poverty, ignorance, injustice and human degradation are the enemies that stand at the gates of civilization? And shall we then, at long last, devote our abundant energies and resources to the conquest of these enemies wherever they exist?

I have enough faith in the American people to answer these questions in the affirmative. I have enough faith in man to believe that he is capable of learning from his mistakes. But, to learn from one's mistakes, one must recognize them; and that is the value of history. Perhaps the reader will find, as I have, that nothing is more fascinating to explore than the history one does not know.

* *Ibid.* Chap. 10 and Appendix A.

SUGGESTED READING

Most scholarly bibliographies are so extensive as to confuse and discourage a would-be student. The following brief list is suggested for those readers of this sketchy outline in whom it may have inspired an appetite for further study.

On India:

Jawaharlal Nehru, *Glimpses of World History*, John Day, New York, 1942. The history of India as related to that of the world, as told to Nehru's daughter in a remarkable series of letters written from prison.

H. N. Brailsford, *Subject India*, John Day, New York, 1943. An Englishman presents the case for India's freedom during the last years of the British raj.

On China:

John King Fairbank, *The United States and China*, Harvard Univ. Press, Cambridge (Mass.), rev. ed., 1958. Free from cumbersome detail and easy to read. Also by Fairbank, *China—The People's Middle Kingdom and the U.S.A.*, Harvard Univ. Press, 1967.

O. Edmund Clubb, *Twentieth-Century China*, Columbia Univ. Press, New York, 1963. Our last consul in Peking tells the complicated story of warlords and early republican China.

Benjamin Schwartz, *Communism and the Rise of Mao*, Harvard Univ. Press, Cambridge (Mass.), 1951. The Communist interpretation of the movement's history.

Edgar Snow, *Red Star over China*, Random House, New York, 1938, a remarkably prescient book; and, by the same author, *The Other Side of the River: Red China Today*, Random House, 1961, in which Snow presents the communist side of the story.

Robert Blum, edited by A. Doak Barnett, *The United States and China in World Affairs*, McGraw-Hill, New York, 1966. A detailed account of the evolution of American policy in Asia and a reasoned plea for its re-examination. Also by Barnett, *Communist China in Perspective*, Praeger, New York, 1962.

On Japan:

Edwin O. Reischauer, *Japan Past and Present*, Knopf, New York, rev. ed., 1964. Comprehensively informative and likewise easy to read.

Fairbank, Reischauer and Albert M. Craig have written a two-volume scholarly and detailed *History of East Asian Civilization*, Houghton Mifflin, Boston, 1965. This authoritative work is not easy to read, but is highly rewarding, covering as it does not only China and Japan but Korea and the peripheral areas.

William W. Lockwood, *The Economic Development of Japan*, Princeton Univ. Press, Princeton (N.J.), 1954 (paperback).

Masao Maruyama, *Thought and Behavior in Modern Japanese Politics*, Oxford Univ. Press, New York, 1963.

Lawrence Olson, *Dimensions of Japan*, American Universities Field Staff, New York, 1963; and *Japan Today and Tomorrow*, Foreign Policy Assn. Headline Series 181, New York, 1966.

* * *

Two authors from whom I have learned and liberally borrowed are:

William H. McNeill, whose history of the human community, *The Rise of the West*, Chicago Univ. Press, Chicago, 1963, superbly narrates in 900 pages the story which I have compressed into a few short chapters.

Michael Rheta Martin, whose *Graphic Guide to World History*, Holt, Rinehart and Winston, New York, 1959, serves as an invaluable aid in coordinating world history.

Both of these works are available in paperback editions and should, in my judgment, be in every school library.

Finally, for those concerned for the future of our country's relations with Asia, I strongly recommend a careful perusal of two documents obtainable from the U.S. Government Printing Office in Washington. They are:

G.P.O. 74 606 O—Testimony of Former Ambassador to the Soviet Union, George F. Kennan, before the Senate Committee on Foreign Relations, January 30, 1967.

G.P.O. 74 686 O—Testimony of Former Ambassador to Japan, Edwin O. Reischauer, before the same Committee on January 31, 1967.

Both documents are interesting, not only because of the content of the prepared statements of the two witnesses but also because the subsequent colloquies between them and the members of the Senate Committee provide a valuable insight into the interplay of varying points of view represented by the interlocutors.

APPENDIX

Concerning Vietnam

On December 31, 1966, I wrote the following letter to *The New York Times*. It was published on January 10, 1967, with the first two sentences deleted. Not knowing whether the letter would appear, I sent copies to my mailing list, asking for comment or criticism.

THE EDITOR, *The New York Times:*

There is an old Greek saying that "whom the gods would destroy they first render mad." And madness seems, indeed, increasingly to take possession of those into whose hands the American people have confided the destiny of their nation. It seems at this moment as if our beloved country were bent upon suicide and upon tearing down in its self-destruction the whole fabric of that human civilization to which it has contributed so much in the past.

The essentially decent and sensible American people do not share this madness but feel powerless to arrest it. They are forced to stand by helplessly, watching their hopes for the meeting of long-neglected public needs dissolve into unfulfilled promises, their nation's substance being wasted, and their sons and brothers being maimed or killed in a brutal war in the making of which they had no part.

To be sure, voices are being raised to demand an end to this all-devouring conflict but, increasingly, these are the voices of men who know of no other way to end it than by doubling and redoubling the stakes in a gamble for total victory through total annihilation.

Until now, this deeply concerned citizen has not favored an outright withdrawal from a commitment unwisely entered into and stretched far beyond the intentions of those who originally made it. But, if the choice is between withdrawal and the ruthless pursuit of total victory, then the time has come to face the issue; for, if that is indeed to be our choice, it is a choice between sanity and madness.

Your newspaper has rendered a great service by exposing upon unimpeachable evidence the cynical brutality and the futility of seeking to bomb North Vietnam into submission, but there is little evidence that your advice to halt this effort will be heeded. In a broader sense, there is little evidence that our government has recognized the arrogance and the folly of seeking to impose a *Pax Americana* upon a world which does not want and will not accept it.

In these circumstances, true patriotism must demand withdrawal from Vietnam, whatever the consequences. Nor will these consequences necessarily injure our national interest, if that interest is truly appraised. As for prestige, our withdrawal will not be seen as a confession of defeat but, rather, as the recognition of a serious error in judgment—an error for which no one leader and no one political party can be held responsible.

It is admittedly not easy for a proud nation to admit a serious mistake in judgment; but, throughout history, great men and great nations have admitted error and become the greater for having done so. And, throughout history, men and nations that have ruthlessly sought total victory by force of arms have ended by being themselves destroyed.

Deerfield Beach, Florida,
December 31, 1966

James P. Warburg

In view of the temper of the times, I had expected at best a mixed reaction, but, of about 250 communications received within a week only one (unsigned) was abusive; four were noncommittal; five offered thoughtful criticism; and more than ninety-five percent expressed unqualified approval.

The most interesting dissent read as follows:

January 12, 1967

I respond at once to your request for comment on your letter of the 31st ulto., to the New York Times. For many years I have applauded your books, pamphlets and letters to the editor, as the voice of our foremost spokesman for the internationally-minded portion of the American people. But, while I still take this view of your spokesmanship, I happen not to agree with your present view on Vietnam.

From the first, I was opposed to our entry into the Vietnam dispute, and I am most earnestly anxious to embrace any feasible plan that can exonerate us from the frightful blunder of our intervention in it. Knowing somewhat of the extraordinary toughness, the unqualified pleasure the war leaders of each faction take in the game of war, their utter disregard for the welfare of the masses, I could see nothing but deep and prolonged trouble for us by intervening in this war. It had seemed

211

to me that our experience in Korea should have taught us a lesson, that we would be well-advised to stay out of Asiatic wars. But apparently that experience was not costly enough. We had to make this second blunder.

I repeat that old maxim: "It was worse than a crime; it was a blunder!" And, as a blunder, the price for it has to be paid in full. There can be no relatively quick or easy way out of it by simply turning our back on it and pulling out.

In the first place, for fourteen years we have encouraged and aided the South Vietnamese to carry on this war. In lives lost, in human welfare sacrificed as the result of our support, they have paid and are continuing to pay a far higher price in human suffering for this war than our country. If we had stayed out of it from the first, the North Vietnamese would long ago have ended the struggle, and the country would have had the kind of totalitarian peace that Communists can bring to a conquered country.

But we have made ourselves their partners and to desert them to their unhappy fate at this late date, to my view, is the kind of bad faith to which I am wholly unwilling to subscribe.

Thus, we are not free to act in our own interest. Having blundered into this war thru our excessive fear of communism, we must resolutely see it through to the end.

There are other reasons, not so persuasive but having real significance, why, as I see it, we cannot unilaterally pull out. I do not urge our loss of prestige by pulling out, tho with many this is a forceful argument. But it does not speed the cause of world peace to have us convince the people of all Asia that Mao and his supporters are quite right in screaming at us "Paper Tiger! Paper Tiger!" How much and for how long would the international air reverberate with that triumphant cry if we were to pull out unilaterally. For, in pulling out, we would abandon far more than South Vietnam. We would leave all Asia at the mercy of Communist China. The huge volume of China's daily accusations against the United States is a testimonial to the restraint we now impose on her conquest, both by subversion and war, of as much of Asia as she could devour, a giant bite at a time . . .

Nor am I persuaded by the starkness with which you put the issue when you say that it is a choice between sanity and madness. This implies that the issue is a very simple one, when, in fact, it is most complex and difficult. You would be more persuasive, I think, if you were to recognize that fact.

There is much, much more to be said on this issue, or complex of issues, but this letter is already too long.

I remain, as always.

Yours in firm and lasting friendship,

To this thoughtful criticism, I replied:

January 16, 1967
Dear Friend and Ally in Many Causes:

I am most grateful for and value highly your thoughtful disagreement with my recent letter to *The New York Times* on the subject of Vietnam. With great respect for your judgment and your expert knowledge of Asia, I welcome the opportunity to reply to your criticism.

We agree about the past. Both of us opposed our entry into the Vietnam dispute. Both of us could foresee nothing but deep and prolonged trouble in military interven-

213

tion. I agree with your citation of the old maxim: "It was worse than a crime; it was a blunder."

However, you say: "The price for the blunder has to be paid in full. There can be no quick or easy way out of it by simply turning our back on it and pulling out." I agree that we have to pay the price for our blunders but we disagree as to what that price is.

You say: "Having blundered into this war through our excessive fear of communism, we must resolutely see it through to the end." To what end? To the total victory demanded by Chairman Rivers of the House Armed Services Committee, who would like to see us "flatten Hanoi and Haiphong and let world opinion go fly a kite?" I do not think you mean that. I think you mean until a decent and honorable peace can be negotiated. If that is correct, I must ask you: "What peace?"

The Geneva Accords of 1954, by which we agreed to abide, did not envisage the permanent partition of Vietnam into two separate countries, one communist and one non-communist; they provided for all-Vietnamese elections in 1956—elections which we prevented because they would have resulted in an overwhelming victory for Ho Chi Minh. (See Eisenhower's memoir). Are we, in your judgment, now honor-bound to see the war through to an end which envisages a permanently partitioned Vietnam, with South Vietnam remaining out of communist control? And, if this is your view, to whom do we owe the accomplishment of this end? To the latest of a series of Saigon governments that have had no roots in popular support? Or to the long-suffering people of South Vietnam? If the latter, do you think the majority want the war to continue until their country can emerge as an independent non-communist nation?

If you do think that this is what the majority of South Vietnamese want, even if it means a protracted war, do you think that there is the slightest chance that North Vietnam will agree to such a peace?

My own view is that a peace settlement on these terms is neither strongly desired by the majority of the South Vietnamese nor acceptable to North Vietnam. It is what *our government* desires in its fear of communist encroachment. My own view is that we *do* have an obligation to those South Vietnamese who have agreed with our government and have fought for such a settlement. The way to meet that obligation is to insist upon an internationally policed political amnesty that will protect these people from assassination or persecution. This should be a *sine qua non* of any peace settlement—or of our withdrawal if no peace settlement can be negotiated.

Let me emphasize that I have not said that we should withdraw *now*. I have contended that we should unconditionally stop bombing North Vietnam and unconditionally accord the National Liberation Front in the South the status of a belligerent in peace negotiations. With this I believe you agree. But, if we do these two things and no peace negotiations result—or, if we persist in our bombing and in our at best ambiguous attitude toward the National Liberation Front, then I say that we shall be faced with the choice between pursuit of total victory or withdrawal upon the sole condition of political amnesty. And I do not apologize for starkly describing this choice as a choice between sanity and madness.

So much for the main thesis of your criticism. You go on to say that there are other reasons, less persuasive but having real significance, why we cannot unilaterally pull out.

You say: "It does not speed the course of world peace to have us convince the people of all Asia that Mao and his supporters are quite right in screaming at us 'Paper Tiger! Paper Tiger!' For, in pulling out, we would abandon far more than North Vietnam. We would leave all Asia at the mercy of Communist China."

I do not doubt that Mao—if he is still in power— would issue triumphant cries if we were to pull out of Vietnam but, after the demonstrated prowess and morale of our armed forces, I doubt whether the cry of "Paper Tiger" would be very convincing. We have clearly demonstrated that the Tiger has claws. By withdrawing, we should merely show that the Tiger, while powerful, is more than a brainless wild beast.

It is true, as you say, that Peking is violently hostile to the United States because it feels hemmed in by our military power. Above all, Peking resents our denying it the possession of Taiwan. But are you sure that China wants to "devour all of Asia"? And, if that is indeed Peking's ambition, whose job is it to prevent such a conquest? Is it ours alone, or is it the job of all nations that desire a peaceful world? If China wants part of the Soviet Union's Asian domain, is that our business? Are we responsible for maintaining India's possession of disputed border territory? I submit that by withdrawing from South Vietnam we should not be "abandoning all of Asia to Chinese conquest." I submit that withdrawal from Vietnam would not mean withdrawal from *our proper share of responsibility* for the maintenance of peace in every part of the world, be it through the United Nations or a concert of powers.

I agree with you that the price for our past blunders must be paid in full. But I suggest that the payment cannot be made in the further brutal pursuit of a meaningless military victory; that it must be paid in confession of error and a more humble appraisement of our great nation's proper role in Asia and throughout the world.

I sign this reply, as you signed your letter, "in firm and lasting friendship" and with profound gratitude for the kind of honest criticism one so rarely receives.

Sincerely,

A few days later, I received the following answer:

I am pleased in every respect with your letter of the 16th. . . . I agree that your quotations from my letter are fair and do not call for a rebuttal from me.

Your letter brings us closer to agreement than I had anticipated, particularly when you say: "Let me emphasize that I have not said we should withdraw *now*."

I look for negotiations to be under way in a year to 18 months. Thus I am not disposed to dictate to General Westmoreland at this moment how he should conduct the war, much as I detest the use of bombing. I would rather see us discussing how far our country should go in these negotiations in order to create peace.

Based upon what information is available, it seems clear that bombing the North has proved itself a failure as well as a major obstacle to peace negotiations, especially with regard to its effect upon the attitude of the Soviet Union. It would seem that a cessation of bombing the North would not materially add to the burdens so magnificently borne by General Westmoreland and his command if his mission were redefined, as suggested by Generals Ridgway and Gavin, to hold key positions rather than to search for and destroy the hostile forces.

POSTSCRIPT

If any proof were needed of the unwisdom of American policy in Southeast Asia, it was provided in June 1967, just as this book was going to press.

Largely because of its involvement in Vietnam, the United States found itself severely handicaped in dealing with a renewed crisis in the Near East where it had vital national interests and a commitment to its honor far more evident than it had ever had in Vietnam.

In 1948 the United States had welcomed, if not actually sponsored, the creation of Israel; both Washington and Moscow had recognized the new state. At the time of the Suez crisis in 1956, Washington and Moscow had acted together to put an end to the conflict, even though the Cold War between them was then at its height. After the Cuban missile crisis of 1962, and the deepening of the Sino-Soviet cleavage, the United States and the Soviet Union both appeared to recognize that they had two things in common: the avoidance of another eyeball-to-eyeball confrontation, and the containment in Asia of a China now hostile to both Russia and the United States.

Until President Johnson repudiated the Southeast Asian policy upon which he had been elected and, in 1965, sent American troops into combat in Vietnam, it seemed as if the Cold War might have ended, as if tensions might continue to relax, and as if Washington and Moscow might, in spite of their differences, pursue somewhat parallel courses in endeavoring to establish more stable world conditions.

This prospect was shattered when President Johnson extended the war into a major American involvement in South Vietnam and then into an attack upon the North; and this at the very moment when the Soviet Premier was in Hanoi presumably seeking to end the conflict.

The deeper the United States became committed in war on the Asian mainland, the greater became the temptation for Moscow to embarrass the United States in other parts of the world. An obvious way to do this was to upset the precarious balance of power in the Near East. It seems probable, as this is written, that Moscow did not wish to incite an actual armed conflict by rearming the Arabs, since such a war might lead to another dangerous great-power confrontation. It seems probable that Nasser broke out of Moscow's control when he demanded the withdrawal of United Nations peace-keeping forces, closed the Gulf of Aqaba to Israeli shipping, and massed his forces in the Sinai peninsula. Whatever Moscow's intentions, this was the time for the United States to act, to reassert the guarantees it had given of Israel's existence and territorial integrity, and to demand strong United Nations action to prevent armed conflict. But the United States was paralyzed by its deep involvement in Vietnam.

And so war came—a war in which Israel might well have been defeated and, unless American promises were fulfilled, exterminated. Had the United States belatedly moved then, no one can say what might have been the result.

Fortunately for the United States and for the world, Israel, outnumbered and surrounded by its enemies, achieved an almost miraculous victory—a victory which saved its existence as a state, saved the United States from a fearful dilemma and, very likely, saved the world for the time being from the outbreak of major war. But the problems of establishing an enduring peace of justice in the Near East remain to be solved and can be solved only by a cooperative effort of all the great powers, including especially the United States and the Soviet Union.

Can such cooperation be achieved, not only in the Near East but in other likely trouble spots, while the United States relentlessly pursues its war in Vietnam?

Note: The substance of this postscript was sent on June 10, 1967, to the *New York Times* as a letter to the editor.

INDEX

225

JAMES P. WARBURG

James P. Warburg is a writer, lecturer and frequent commentator on world affairs, well known both here and abroad. In 1932, as one of Wall Street's youngest bank presidents, he was summoned to Washington by Franklin D. Roosevelt as a financial adviser. He declined a Cabinet post, but participated actively in the First Hundred Days of the New Deal and attended the ill-fated World Economic Conference in London, summoned to Washington by Franklin D. Roosevelt Administration. He returned to serve during World War II as the official in change of American propaganda policy in the European Theater. Since 1945 he has devoted himself to the cause of world peace. Mr. Warburg's home is in Greenwich, Connecticut. He is a member of the Council on Foreign Relations in New York and of the Commission to Study the Organization of Peace. A former director of the American Academy of Political and Social Science, he is now a trustee of the Institute for Policy Studies in Washington.